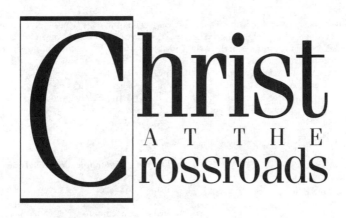

Christ AT THE Crossroads

BIBLE STUDY GUIDE

From the Bible-teaching ministry of

Charles R. Swindoll

INSIGHT FOR LIVING

Chuck graduated in 1963 from Dallas Theological Seminary, where he now serves as the school's fourth president, helping to prepare a new generation of men and women for the ministry. Chuck has served in pastorates in three states: Massachusetts, Texas, and California, including almost twenty-three years at the First Evangelical Free Church in Fullerton, California. His sermon messages have been aired over radio since 1979 as the *Insight for Living* broadcast. A best-selling author, Chuck has written numerous books and booklets on many subjects.

Based on the outlines and transcripts of Chuck's sermons, the study guide text is co-authored by Lee Hough, a graduate of the University of Texas at Arlington and Dallas Theological Seminary.

Editor in Chief:
Cynthia Swindoll

Coauthor of Text:
Lee Hough

Assistant Editor:
Wendy Peterson

Senior Copy Editors:
Deborah Gibbs
Glenda Schlahta

Copy Editor:
Marco Salazar

Typographer:
Bob Haskins

Director, Communications Division:
Deedee Snyder

Project Manager:
Alene Cooper

Project Coordinator:
Susan Nelson

Assistant Production Manager:
John Norton

Unless otherwise identified, all Scripture references are from the New American Standard Bible, © The Lockman Foundation 1960, 1962, 1963, 1968, 1971, 1972, 1973, 1975, 1977. Used by permission. Other translations cited are *J. B. Phillips: The New Testament in Modern English* [PHILLIPS] and the *New King James Version* [NKJV].

An effort has been made to locate sources and obtain permission where necessary for the quotations used in this book. In the event of any unintentional omission, a modification will gladly be incorporated in future printings.

ISBN 1-57972-090-0
COVER DESIGN: Gary V. Lett
Printed in the United States of America

CONTENTS

* These messages were not a part of the original series but are compatible with it.

INTRODUCTION

Throughout my ministry I have emphasized that our Lord never leaves His people in the lurch. He neither walks away from us nor keeps Himself at a distance when tough times come. On the contrary, He stays near, He cares, He comforts, He ministers to us deeply and compassionately, particularly when we arrive at life's crossroads and must decide which way to turn.

This series is about Christ's presence in our lives at those times when we are hard-pressed, squeezed into a corner, and unsure about the next step. Hopefully, each study will bring you reassurance . . . life's crossroads can be very painful and confusing.

One of Webster's definitions of *crossroad* is "a crucial point especially where a decision must be made." Perhaps you find yourself there today. If not, you probably will some day in the future. My hope—really, my primary motivation for these messages—is that you will

- realize you are not alone,

- discover specific scriptural guidelines that will bring encouragement and discernment, and

- gain new strength to endure.

If these three objectives are accomplished, I will feel our time together will have not been in vain, as you will have a better perspective on the direction you should take at the crossroads in your own life.

Chuck Swindoll

PUTTING TRUTH
INTO ACTION

Knowledge apart from application falls short of God's desire for His children. He wants us to apply what we learn so that we will change and grow. This study guide was prepared with these goals in mind. As you go through the following pages, we hope your desire to discover biblical truth will grow as your understanding of God's Word increases, and that you will be encouraged to apply what you've learned.

To assist you in your study, we've included a section called Living Insights at the end of each lesson. These exercises will challenge you to study further and to think of specific ways to put your discoveries into action.

There are many ways to use this guide—in personal devotions, group studies, discussions with friends and family, and Sunday school classes. And, of course, it's an ideal study aid when you're listening to its corresponding "Insight for Living" radio series.

To benefit most from this study guide, we would encourage you to consider it a spiritual journal. That's why we've included space in the Living Insights for recording your thoughts and discoveries. We hope you'll return to those sections often for review and encouragement as you continue to grow in your walk with Christ.

Lee Hough
Coauthor of Text
Author of Living Insights

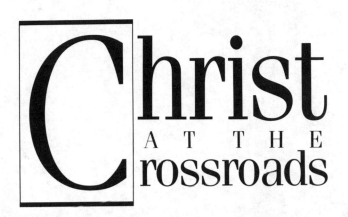

Chapter 1
CHRIST AT THE CROSSROAD OF TEMPTATION
Matthew 4:1–11

Remember Robert Frost's proverbial fork in the road?

Two roads diverged in a yellow wood,
And sorry I could not travel both
And be one traveler, long I stood
And looked down one as far as I could
To where it bent in the undergrowth;

Then took the other, as just as fair,
And having perhaps the better claim,
Because it was grassy and wanted wear;
Though as for that the passing there
Had worn them really about the same,

And both that morning equally lay
In leaves no step had trodden black.
Oh, I kept the first for another day!
Yet knowing how way leads on to way,
I doubted if I should ever come back.

I shall be telling this with a sigh
Somewhere ages and ages hence:
Two roads diverged in a wood, and I—
I took the one less traveled by,
And that has made all the difference.[1]

1. Robert Frost, "The Road Not Taken," in *Poems That Live Forever*, comp. Hazel Felleman (New York, N.Y.: Doubleday, 1965), p. 317.

More than a pleasant rhyme about a walk in the woods, "The Road Not Taken" is a beautiful metaphor about crossroads, critical junctures that necessitate life-changing decisions. Some we prepare for as they approach, like a marriage, a career, or a move to a new home. Others, perhaps even most, intersect our lives unexpectedly, like the sudden news of marital infidelity, or the loss of a job, a child, or good health.

How do we make wise decisions at such crucial times? How do we maintain our equilibrium when we've been broadsided by bad news? No one knows how better than the man who endured constant beatings, imprisonments, and danger—the apostle Paul.

Life's Inevitable Crossroads

Like Robert Frost, Paul came to a crucial fork in his life. One where he was suddenly blinded with the crossroads decision to either continue persecuting Christians or become one himself (Acts 9). Paul chose the road less traveled by, the straight-and-narrow path of faith in Christ, and that made all the difference. Years later, in a letter to the church at Philippi, the Apostle explained how he had since learned to handle life's crossroads in any circumstance.

> I have learned to be content in whatever circumstances I am. I know how to get along with humble means, and I also know how to live in prosperity; in any and every circumstance I have learned the secret of being filled and going hungry, both of having abundance and suffering need. I can do all things through Him who strengthens me. (Phil. 4:11b–13)

Whatever the crossroad, Paul found Christ was always there, always willing to strengthen and guide him on his journey down the road less traveled. And the same is still true for us today.

As we begin our study of several crossroads in Christ's life and ministry, let's discover how to make Paul's words—"I can do all things through Christ"—our own. Then we, too, will be able to look back ages and ages hence and say with a contented sigh that it has made all the difference.

Jesus' Encounter with the Tempter

Our study begins with a crucial juncture in Jesus' life as recorded in Matthew 4.

2

The Setting

About the time Christ turned thirty, this carpenter from Galilee gave His tools away, hugged His family, and headed for the Jordan River in Judea. There He knew He would find the prophet who was preparing the way for His public ministry—His wonderful, agonizing journey to the Cross.

No one knew the enormity of the Messiah's journey better than Satan. Nor was there anyone who wanted more to stop Him. For the Evil One knew that Christ's death and resurrection would seal his ultimate doom. So immediately following Jesus' baptism (Matt. 3), the adversary tries to detour Christ at the crossroad of temptation.

> Then Jesus was led up by the Spirit into the wilderness to be tempted by the devil. And after He had fasted forty days and forty nights, He then became hungry.[2] (Matt. 4:1–2)

Satan is hungry too. The apostle Peter describes him as a roaring lion, prowling about for someone to devour (1 Pet. 5:8). And at this particular time, that someone is Christ. But notice that the devil doesn't attack Jesus immediately after His baptism. He waits until the Son of Man is alone, in a wilderness, weakened from more than a month of fasting. Then the stalking lion pounces.

The Temptations

Satan's attack on Christ, however, is not like the savage and bloody ones made by lions in nature. Rather, he makes a more subtle attack, attempting to bring his prey down with three temptations, each ruthlessly designed to lure the Savior away from His Father and His mission.

First test: of a personal nature. Drawing upon what God called Jesus at His baptism—"My beloved Son"—Satan dares Christ to prove His identity with an appetizing display of power.

> And the tempter came and said to Him, "If You are the Son of God, command that these stones become bread." (Matt. 4:3)

---

2. Though normally used to connote being seduced toward evil, the Greek term for "tempted," *peirazō*, in Matthew 4:1 suggests more the idea of being tested for the purpose of approving or affirming. Another example of the same use of this word is found in Genesis 22:1.

Christ certainly has the power to accept the dare. He has a powerful physical hunger too. So what would be wrong with turning a few stones into bread? Everything. Hidden beneath Satan's seemingly harmless challenge is a snare. The devil is testing Christ to see whether He can be lured into using His power for selfish purposes. Instead of waiting on the Father to meet His needs, can Jesus be tempted to satisfy Himself, do His own thing? If so, perhaps Jesus would prefer to feed the world rather than die for it; be a Bread King to the hungry rather than the Bread of Life to the lost (John 6:35).

> But He answered and said, "It is written, 'Man shall
> not live on bread alone, but on every word that
> proceeds out of the mouth of God.'" (Matt. 4:4)

Hungry as He is, Christ passes up the tempting bread of immediate satisfaction for the more lasting food of obeying the Father. Satan's first crossroad is bypassed. Up ahead, however, literally way up, loom still two more.

Second test: of a public nature. From a perch forty-five stories high, the devil next attempts to goad Jesus into showing off His identity with a sensational leap.

> Then the devil took Him into the holy city; and he
> had Him stand on the pinnacle of the temple, and
> said to Him, "If You are the Son of God throw Your-
> self down; for it is written,
> 'He will give His angels charge concerning
> You';
> and
> 'On their hands they will bear You up,
> Lest You strike Your foot against a stone.'"
> (vv. 5–6)

It all sounds so . . . so sensible—and intriguing. Just imagine, what a breathtaking way to inaugurate a public ministry! The jump would be spectacular, a real crowd pleaser. One that would surely establish Jesus as the Messiah the Jews expected to suddenly come down from the sky to His temple (Mal. 3:1).

But Jesus isn't interested in pleasing Satan or crowds with death-defying feats. His only concern is to please His Father.

> Jesus said to him, "On the other hand, it is written,
> 'You shall not put the Lord your God to the test.'"
> (Matt. 4:7)

What's wrong with a little pinnacle-jumping now and then if it would demonstrate God's power? It's called *presumption:* flirting with danger to prove power. And the Scriptures condemn this as sin.

God sometimes expects His children to take risks of faith. But He never condones using sensational recklessness in order to show off divine deliverance. To do so only draws attention to ourselves instead of to God and creates a circus atmosphere where greater and greater miracles are sought in order to hold the crowd.[3]

Would Jesus have survived had He flirted with danger and jumped? Yes. His life would have been preserved, but not His mission. The test was to see if He would draw all people to Himself by relying on sensationalism—"Come see the one and only leaping, miracle Messiah make His most spectacular jump yet!"—or the way of the Cross. Jesus chose the Cross. And Satan? He decided to pull out all the stops and make the third test his most extraordinary one.

Third test: of a power nature. With the flair of a circus ringmaster, that consummate showman Satan parades everything he has in one last effort to woo Christ from the Cross.

> Again, the devil took Him to a very high mountain, and showed Him all the kingdoms of the world, and their glory; and he said to Him, "All these things will I give You, if You fall down and worship me."
> (vv. 8–9)

Now remember, Jesus hasn't begun His ministry yet. He doesn't even have a single follower. And He knows that the task ahead will be murderously difficult. *But it needn't be.* Satan's willing to hand Him the world He's been sent to save on a silver platter. No suffering, no struggling, no sacrifice. Just one little compromise and this world and the crown of power that goes with it are all His.

Then what's the problem? It bypasses the Cross. God wants His Son to rule over all the kingdoms of the world, not with a crown of power given by the enemy, but with a crown of thorns worn on a Cross.

So despite all the allure of glitter and glamour, this lone, hungry ex-carpenter from Galilee will not be swayed from obeying the

---

3. Think of the two preachers who, after surviving poisonous snake bites, decided to put their faith to an even greater test by drinking strychnine. But this wasn't a test of faith—it was pinnacle-jumping presumption at its worst. Both died a few hours later. (As told by Charles R. Swindoll, in *Growing Strong in the Seasons of Life* [Portland, Oreg.: Multnomah Press, 1983], p. 342).

Father or fulfilling His mission. And He tells Satan as much with a sure and direct command.

> Then Jesus said to him, "Begone, Satan! For it is written, 'You shall worship the Lord your God, and serve Him only.'" (v. 10)

The Outcome

Frustrated and angry at his failure, Satan departs (v. 11). The crossroad of temptation he planned for Jesus turns out to be only a crossroad of defeat for himself. Luke adds in his gospel account that the devil didn't leave for good, however, but "departed from Him until an opportune time" (Luke 4:13b). Though the roaring lion failed to devour the Lamb of God, he did not give up. The hunter simply resumed stalking, watching for another moment to pounce.

When Temptation Crosses Our Path

Temptation stalks us all. And though we may not be able to stop it from attacking, we can resist and elude its grip. Here are three practical suggestions to take with you so that the next time temptation strikes, you will be able to stand and resist as Christ did.

First: Don't Be Alarmed . . . Expect It!

The more you expect temptation, the less alarmed you'll be by all of its prowling and growling. None of us are free from its presence. It roams in the minds of even the holiest of saints. And though none of us can actually see it or touch it, we can prepare for this invisible marauder by adopting a watchful attitude. Temptations aren't nearly as dangerous when nothing they can do surprises you anymore.

Second: Don't Be Blind . . . Detect It!

Whether Satan is directly behind it or not, temptation has innumerable methods of attack, few of which are easy to detect. So stay alert; watch for signs; become a skilled tracker who can spot temptations before they have a chance to strike.

Third: Don't Be Clever . . . Reject It!

There's a name for those who flirt with temptation: Victim! It will devour anyone who dares toy with it, the same as any real lion would in the wild. Temptation is not something you can play with.

You can never take the killer instinct out of it and make it your pet. But you can learn how to protect yourself as Christ did by meeting this enemy head-on with God's written Word (Ps. 119:9–11).

In Conclusion

Are you facing a particular crossroad of temptation right now? Do you feel too weak to resist? Remember this: Christ knows what it's like to be hit with the full brunt of the enemy's attack. He survived Satan's hardest tests, and He can strengthen you to do the same. The author of Hebrews offers these comforting words.

> Since then we have a great high priest who has passed through the heavens, Jesus the Son of God, let us hold fast our confession. For we do not have a high priest who cannot sympathize with our weaknesses, but one who has been tempted in all things as we are, yet without sin. Let us therefore draw near with confidence to the throne of grace, that we may receive mercy and may find grace to help in time of need. (4:14–16)

Two roads diverged in a wood, and I? I remembered I can do all things through Christ— Christ at the crossroads. And that has made all the difference.

 Living Insights

In *West with the Night*, an extraordinary autobiography about growing up in Africa, Beryl Markham tells the story of Paddy—a wild, solitary lion that adopted a neighbor's farm as his home. For a twelve-mile radius, this oversized cat wandered "through Elkington's fields and pastures like an affable, if apostrophic, emperor, a-stroll in the gardens of his court."[4] His seeming affability, however, proved to be deceptive one day, as young Beryl found out.

> I was within twenty yards of the Elkington lion before I saw him. He lay sprawled in the morning sun, huge, black-maned, and gleaming with life. His

---

4. Beryl Markham, *West with the Night* (1942; reprint, San Francisco, Calif.: North Point Press, 1983), p. 59.

7

tail moved slowly, stroking the rough grass like a knotted rope end. His body was sleek and easy, making a mould where he lay, a cool mould, that would be there when he had gone. He was not asleep; he was only idle. He was rusty-red, and soft, like a strokable cat.

I stopped and he lifted his head with magnificent ease and stared at me out of yellow eyes. . . .

I remembered the rules that one remembers. I did not run. I walked very slowly, and I began to sing a defiant song.

'Kali coma Simba sisi,' I sang, 'Asikari yoti ni udari!—Fierce like the lion are we, Askari all are brave!'

I went in a straight line past Paddy when I sang it, seeing his eyes shine in the thick grass, watching his tail beat time to the metre of my ditty. . . .

Singing it still, I took up my trot toward the rim of the low hill which might, if I were lucky, have Cape gooseberry bushes on its slopes.

The country was grey-green and dry, and the sun lay on it closely, making the ground hot under my bare feet. There was no sound and no wind.

Even Paddy made no sound, coming swiftly behind me.

What I remember most clearly of the moment that followed are three things—a scream that was barely a whisper, a blow that struck me to the ground, and . . . Paddy's teeth close on the flesh of my leg.[5]

What happened to Beryl can happen to us all at the crossroad of temptation. The lion we face there, like Paddy, is also silent and swift, and its attacks can be just as deadly. But unlike the lion that left its scars on Beryl, our adversary is invisible and insidiously patient. Satan doesn't try to bring our whole life down in one charge; rather, he prefers to fall upon his prey in subtle ways, constantly weakening and wearing us down blow by blow, little bite by little bite. Then he comes in for an easy kill.

5. Markham, *West with the Night*, pp. 61–63.

Are there any "little" temptations trying to nibble away your honesty? Purity? Or some other area? There's your crossroad of temptation. Our fall isn't usually when we commit some sin that all the world sees. Long before then, the hidden places of our hearts are where the crossroad decisions are made that ultimately shape our lives. Using the space provided, try to identify these subtle, vulnerable areas where you're being tempted and try to discern how it's happening.

Where: _____

How: _____

_____

Where: _____

How: _____

_____

Where: _____

How: _____

_____

These temptations may look small to you now, but each time you give in to them they grow stronger and bigger and harder to tame until someday they may just eat you alive. So don't turn your back on them as if they weren't there. Stop them now!

 Living Insights

When it comes to temptations, we all know our weaknesses, don't we? So naturally we tend to guard our hearts diligently in those areas. But while the battle rages in the trenches of our weaknesses, it may just be that temptation is gaining a foothold in our strengths. Commentator William Barclay warns:

> We must always remember that again and again we are tempted *through our gifts*. The person who is gifted with charm will be tempted to use that charm

"to get away with anything." The person who is gifted with the power of words will be tempted to use his command of words to produce glib excuses to justify his own conduct. The person with a vivid and sensitive imagination will undergo agonies of temptation that a more stolid person will never experience. The person with great gifts of mind will be tempted to use these gifts for himself and not for others, to become the master and not the servant of men. It is the grim fact of temptation that it is just where we are strongest that we must be for ever on the watch.[6]

In what ways has the Lord gifted you?

_____

_____

_____

_____

_____

What are some of the temptations prompted by these gifts?

_____

_____

_____

_____

For further help in understanding about temptation, study James 1:13–15 and read C. S. Lewis' classic *The Screwtape Letters.*

6. William Barclay, *The Gospel of Matthew,* rev. ed., The Daily Study Bible Series (Philadelphia, Pa.: Westminster Press, 1975), vol. 1, p. 66.

Chapter 2

CHRIST AT THE CROSSROAD OF MISUNDERSTANDING

Mark 3:1–6, 20–26, 30–35

Seat belts and air bags have gone a long way toward protecting lives in collisions. But there's no patented safety device that will protect us in one of life's most common collisions—misunderstandings.

They can happen anywhere at anytime. Someone misjudges our motives or misreads our actions, and it can take days, months, even years to repair the damage. Provided, of course, that the relationship wasn't completely totaled to begin with . . . or that either party involved was a hockey player.

Didn't you know? Hockey players love collisions. That's why the game was invented. Well, at least that's what it looks like. In theory, the game's about two teams of six players on ice skates trying to make a goal by driving a three-inch rubber puck into the opponent's net. In reality, however, it's more like a game of legalized collisions for people who love slamming into one another!

Sure there's skill, strategy, even a certain gracefulness; but when two of those enormously misshapen players collide—such a mild word for two people trying to decapitate one another—things can get ugly in a hurry. You know it's bad when the players' gloves come off. That's the signal for both benches to swarm onto the ice like killer bees and converge into an angry pile of numbers. The fists of number 47 are pounding 3's face, who's tearing 50's jersey, who's kicking 13, who's choking 65, who is pulling 74's face off along with his mask. About the only thing they don't do to each other is bite, and that's because none of them have any teeth!

Hockey players or no, we've all experienced misunderstandings like that. One minute we're gliding along, life is great, and the next, someone hits us head-on, the gloves fly, and all rules are off. Both benches of family and friends rush into the fray, and there's every manner of verbal punching, kicking, and sometimes biting—enough so that it would scare even a hockey player!

Misunderstood? You Are Not Alone

Let's briefly look at just a few of the ways these collisions occur.

11

Examples from Life

Have you ever been misunderstood when you reached out to help someone in need? You offered a little assistance only to find out that the person who smiled and thanked you later told a friend they thought you acted like a nosy busybody.

Or did you ever try to *gently* restore a close Christian friend who was wandering from the faith? You approached them with a humble and understanding heart, but all this other person could see or hear was that you were being harsh and judgmental.

And what about the time your wife fixed that succulent roast—remember? You liked it so much that you asked, "Where did you buy this?" Now, you meant this as a friendly question, a kind of indirect way of affirming her cooking. But she took it as a criticism and immediately went on the defensive: "What's wrong with it? You know, I'm getting pretty sick and tired of fixing meals that nobody appreciates." "But I *like* this roast," you pleaded. "Forget it," she snipped, "It's too late, the meal's ruined." And indeed it was.

Makes you wince, doesn't it? We can all probably remember a meal, an evening, or a special day that was ruined by some innocuous statement taken the wrong way. And while most misunderstandings are easily cleared up, some, like the ones in Joseph's and David's lives, linger for years and result in mistreatment.

Examples from Scripture

Joseph grew up in a family knotted with misunderstandings. Eventually, they led to a confrontation with his brothers in which Joseph was bound and sold as a slave to Potiphar, an Egyptian official. In time, Joseph was elevated to the position of overseer in charge of all his master's possessions. It was while he was in that position that Potiphar's wife repeatedly tried to seduce him. When words wouldn't sway him, she literally grabbed Joseph and tried to pull him to her. But Joseph fled, leaving his garment clutched in her hands. Enraged by his refusal, Mrs. Potiphar screamed rape, Mr. Potiphar believed her, and Joseph spent the next two years in prison because of a misunderstanding.

Joseph's mistreatment was harsh, but harsher still was the mistreatment David received at the hands of King Saul. At first, the king loved the shepherd boy whose skillful harp could soothe his tormented heart. Saul was even delighted when David defeated Goliath and routed the Philistines. But it wasn't long afterward that Saul misconstrued David's successes as an attempt to take the throne.

So the king turned on the one person who, ironically, was his most devoted servant.

It began with Saul throwing a spear at David during one of his raving fits. Then he tried to have him killed in battle. Finally, the king dropped all pretenses and ordered David to be executed. From king's confidant and warrior to social outcast and criminal, David spent the next twelve years hiding in caves, always on the move, eluding the pointed spears of Saul's mistaken jealousy.

Misunderstandings that last for a day or a week can feel like a lifetime. But twelve years? It's hard to imagine.

There is One who can imagine, though; Someone whose conception, death, and everything in between was wrapped in misunderstandings. His undeserved pain and suffering didn't simply feel like it lasted a lifetime, it did.

Misunderstood? Meet Him Who Understands

The most misunderstood individual who ever lived was Jesus Christ. Critics joked about His birth, tittering about illegitimacy. They disputed His heavenly origin with ethnic jeers and taunts that He belonged to the Devil. They scorned His purpose and condemned His teachings. And in the end, these same people crucified Him as a criminal.

The apostle John wrote, "The light shines in the darkness, and the darkness did not comprehend it" (John 1:5). Christ collided with this uncomprehending darkness every day at just about every turn. For a glimpse of what it must have been like, let's turn to Mark 3.

Misunderstood by the Pharisees

Christ's heavenly light blazed as He helped and healed others. But even then He was misunderstood, especially by the religious leaders whose hatred eclipsed their understanding.

> And He entered again into a synagogue; and a man was there with a withered hand. And they were watching Him to see if He would heal him on the Sabbath, in order that they might accuse Him. (vv. 1–2)

The Pharisees were rule makers, consummate legalists. They loved handing out photocopies of all the exacting do's and don'ts they added to the Law of Moses. Important rules, such as women not being allowed to look in a mirror on the Sabbath because they

13

might discover a gray hair and commit the grievous sin of plucking it out! They had another rule, one that prohibited healing on the Sabbath unless the situation was life threatening. Christ knew about this rule, and He knew that breaking it was punishable by death; but He also knew that "the Sabbath was made for man, and not man for the Sabbath" (2:27). So

> He said to the man with the withered hand, "Rise and come forward!" And He said to [the Pharisees], "Is it lawful on the Sabbath to do good or to do harm, to save a life or to kill?" But they kept silent. And after looking around at them with anger, grieved at their hardness of heart, He said to the man, "Stretch out your hand." And he stretched it out, and his hand was restored. (3:3–5)

Jesus' question cut right to the heart of the Law, something the Pharisees had never touched with all their rules. And for the first time in years, the true light of God's Sabbath shone in that synagogue. But only the man with the restored hand felt it. Only those with an open heart saw it. But the withered hearts of the Pharisees made it impossible for them to see or feel anything but a murderous hatred.

> And the Pharisees went out and immediately began taking counsel with the Herodians against Him, as to how they might destroy Him. (v. 6)

Misunderstood by His Own People

Jesus' second crossroad of misunderstanding is found a little further down in verse 20.

> And He came home, and the multitude gathered again, to such an extent that they could not even eat a meal.

When Christ returned to His hometown,[1] such an enormous following came with Him that He became completely absorbed in ministering to them.[2] Now imagine for a moment what the scuttlebutt

---

1. It's impossible to know whether this was Nazareth, where Jesus was reared, or Capernaum, the place that later became His adopted home.

2. To appreciate just how large the crowd must have been, read Mark 1:28, 32–33; 2:2, 13.

was among some of the older hometown folks. "Say, what's the ruckus? What are all these people doing here?" "Haven't you heard? Jesus is back." "Isn't he the fellow who quit his day job to be some sort of preacher?" "Yep." "I hear he's got fishermen and tax gatherers for disciples." "Uh huh, and they say he's made the Pharisees fighting mad." "He must be crazy!" "Well, what would you expect from someone who doesn't eat." "Doesn't eat?" "That's right. Benjamin said that Nathanael heard that Jesus hasn't had a bite since he hit town. Too busy preaching and all." "Now I know he's crazy. Somebody better go talk some sense into that religious fanatic before he embarrasses us all!"

Sound farfetched? Read what Mark wrote.

> And when His own people heard of this, they went out to take custody of Him; for they were saying, "He has lost His senses." (v. 21)

First the Pharisees plotted to kill Jesus because they misunderstood His actions. Now the hometown crowd is trying to put Jesus away because they have mistaken His passion for insanity. What next? The scribes. They misunderstand Jesus' power and accuse Him of being demon possessed.

Misunderstood by the Scribes

According to verse 22, a delegation of expert attorneys in the Law, called scribes, were dispatched from Jerusalem to investigate Jesus. Here's what they officially concluded:

> "He is possessed by Beelzebul," and "He casts out the demons by the ruler of the demons." (v. 22b)

Jesus couldn't stop the Pharisees from plotting His death or keep old acquaintances from thinking He was crazy. But let these so-called experts in the Law argue such a blasphemous misconception that His power was from Satan? No. This Jesus would not allow. And He made short work of them, pointing out the stupidity behind their accusation.

> And He called them to Himself and began speaking to them in parables, "How can Satan cast out Satan? And if a kingdom is divided against itself, that kingdom cannot stand. And if a house is divided against itself, that house will not be able to stand. And if

Satan has risen up against himself and is divided, he cannot stand, but he is finished!" (vv. 23–26)

Case closed. But there still remains one more misunderstanding on this chapter's docket. The last collision to be examined is perhaps the one that pains us most—being misunderstood by family.

Misunderstood by His Family

Few situations hit as hard as what happened to Christ next.

And His mother and His brothers arrived, and standing outside they sent word to Him, and called Him. (v. 31)

Most Bible scholars agree that the reason Jesus' family waited outside and called for Him is because they were convinced He had lost His mind. They wanted to talk some sense into Jesus, maybe convince Him to take back His old job at the carpentry shop and stop all this foolishness about being God's Messiah.

Scripture doesn't say how deeply it hurt Christ to be misunderstood by His mother and brothers. Perhaps it doesn't really need to. What it does record is Jesus' gentle way of turning His family's misunderstanding into an opportunity to assert His kinship with all those who do the will of God.

And a multitude was sitting around Him, and they said to Him, "Behold, Your mother and Your brothers are outside looking for You." And answering them, He said, "Who are My mother and My brothers?" And looking about on those who were sitting around Him, He said, "Behold, My mother and My brothers! For whoever does the will of God, he is My brother and sister and mother." (vv. 32–35)

Misunderstood? Here's Help to Get You Through

In almost every family circle, among almost every circle of friends, misunderstandings exist that eat away at relationships like acid. And the longer they're left unattended, the more corrosive they become. So the next time you're misunderstood and you need help dealing with it, try asking yourself these three practical questions.

First, when a misunderstanding occurs, ask *who*. Consider the source. Try to see things from the other person's perspective. It will enable you to handle the situation with a greater sense of equity and patience. Second, if it continues, ask *why*. Examine the reason. Could it be something that you're doing without realizing it? A blind spot perhaps? Or is the other person just given to negativism? Third, as it ends, ask *what*. Learn the lessons. In what way can you profit from this experience? Did you learn something about yourself that needs changing?

Questions of who, why, and what are useless, however, without forgiveness. Forgiveness must occur when there's been a collision in a relationship over some misunderstanding. It doesn't necessarily mean you agree or will be able to restore the relationship to its previous level of intimacy. Paul and Barnabas clashed over John Mark and ended up going separate ways, but there was still forgiveness.

When we withhold forgiveness—and we do that more than any of us like to admit—we become prisoners in our own self-made cells of bitterness. We think we're exacting revenge on this other person, when in reality, our bitterness is taking its revenge on us. We're the ones who suffer, whose capacity to love is diminished.

Emerson wrote, "To be great is to be misunderstood."[3] To be greater, however, is to forgive the one who misunderstood. Jesus was not only the greatest man to ever live, but also the most misunderstood, and the most forgiving, even as He hung unjustly on the cross (Luke 23:34). Trusting in Him doesn't protect us from being hit with misunderstandings, but it will enable us to survive them, to repair the damage, and to heal the wounds through forgiveness.

 Living Insights   STUDY ONE

In his excellent book *Forgive and Forget*, Lewis Smedes grapples with tough issues spawned by misunderstandings. Issues like whether or not to forgive people who refuse to admit they are wrong.

> When someone hurts us meanly, we want him to suffer too. We expect this clod to pay his dues; we want him to grovel a little. The old-fashioned word for what we want is *repentance*.
>
> But the people who hurt us do not always come through.

3. Ralph Waldo Emerson, as quoted in *The Oxford Dictionary of Quotations*, 3d ed. (1979; reprint, Oxford, England: Oxford University Press, 1980), p. 207.

The question is: should we forgive them anyway? Does it even make sense to forgive someone who would rather we keep our forgiveness and feed it to the dog?[4]

Is there someone in your life on whom you'd love to sic your well-fed dog? A friend? A coworker? A family member? Someone who, like Potiphar with Joseph or Saul with David, has misunderstood and mistreated you without the slightest tinge of remorse?

Write down their name: _____

Will you forgive this person anyway? If you're like most, each time the thought occurs, your sense of justice violently objects, "But it's not fair!" And it isn't. This other person doesn't deserve to be forgiven. But what about what's fair to you? Have you thought about that lately? Perhaps Lewis Smedes can help.

> Recall the pain of being wronged, the hurt of being stung, cheated, demeaned. Doesn't the memory of it fuel the fire of fury again, reheat the pain again, make it hurt again? Suppose you never forgive, suppose you feel the hurt each time your memory lights on the people who did you wrong. And suppose you have a compulsion to think of them constantly. You have become a prisoner of your past pain; you are locked into a torture chamber of your own making. . . .
>
> The only way to heal the pain that will not heal itself is to forgive the person who hurt you. Forgiving stops the reruns of pain. . . .
>
> When you release the wrongdoer from the wrong, you cut a malignant tumor out of your inner life.
>
> You set a prisoner free, but you discover that the real prisoner was yourself.[5]

Are you tired of doing hard time for an injustice you didn't commit? Then forgive this other person and set yourself free. That's fair, isn't it?[6]

---

4. Lewis B. Smedes, *Forgive and Forget: Healing the Hurts We Don't Deserve* (New York, N.Y.: Pocket Books, 1984), p. 89.

5. Smedes, *Forgive and Forget*, p. 170.

6. Does forgiving others who won't admit they are wrong mean we're excusing their sin, tolerating it, trivializing it? No! Absolutely not. To really understand what forgiveness is and is not, we highly recommend Smedes' book *Forgive and Forget*.

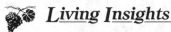

We could talk about all the ways we've been misunderstood, and no doubt there've been plenty. However, we need to balance our focus and consider the possibility, "Who have I misunderstood and treated unfairly?"

Have _you_ ever told someone to keep their forgiveness and feed it to the dog, only to find out later that they were right and you were wrong?

Who? _____

What have you done about it? Here's what most of us do: instead of asking for forgiveness, we start rationalizing—"Well, everybody makes mistakes." We try toning down the really hateful things we said so that we won't feel so guilty—"I'm sure she's had worse insults about her weight." It's true! We do that. And we keep doing it, oftentimes, until we reach a tolerable level of guilt which doesn't demand that we seek forgiveness. So we act as if nothing ever happened and expect the other person to do the same.

It would be a strange prodigal son who returned to his father and, instead of saying, "Father, I have sinned against heaven and in your sight," said, "Hey Pop! Great to see you. Let me get out of these rags and let's you and I have dinner. How's Mom?"

Is that what you're doing? Are you unwilling to admit your own sinfulness yet wanting others to come crawling to you confessing theirs? I hope you said yes, because all of us are like that. Let's admit it and get on with the business of also acknowledging the hard truth that we've misjudged others and need to ask their forgiveness. Don't wait. Don't put it off. Do it now. Use the space below to write out what wrongs need confessing and the soonest possible time you can meet with the person you have hurt.

_____

_____

_____

_____

Oh, and one more thing. If they have a dog, you might want to call and let them know when and _why_ you're coming! God bless.

Chapter 3

CHRIST AT THE CROSSROAD
OF ANXIETY

Luke 10:38–42

Are you anxious? Really anxious? What you need is a comma. No, on second thought, if you're that anxious, you probably need something stronger like a semicolon or a period. Of course, you could go for an exclamation point, but that would be pushing things, don't you think?

Perhaps it would help if we backed up and let David Runcorn, author of *A Center of Quiet*, explain what we're talking about.

> If you have a magazine or newspaper handy, try reading any article without using the punctuation marks. It doesn't make much sense does it? It all becomes a hectic string of words. The meaning is lost. It lacks direction. The purpose of punctuation in a piece of writing is to guide the reader into the true meaning of the words and phrases; through it we understand. Punctuation also gives life and purpose to the words.[1]

For many of us, our lives resemble an article without punctuation. There are no pauses for prayer, no commas or full stops of silence or solitude, just one hectic string of worries that hound us from one activity to the next. Even now, as we begin this study, they are there, distracting, agitating.

Tight finances, debt, divorce rebelliouschildrenabuseimmorality guiltlonelinessshamegriefdepressiondiseasepain-*and*-lots more, all at once, without stop. Need a comma?

We all do. So let's slow our pace and insert a pause here—now. We can do that by offering up a prayer together, like the one Peter Marshall wrote about releasing tension. Pray through it once, slowly, then personalize the prayer by inserting the pronouns *I* and *me* where appropriate and repeat it a second time.

---

1. David Runcorn, *A Center of Quiet: Hearing God When Life Is Noisy* (Downers Grove, Ill.: InterVarsity Press, 1990), p. 5.

Father, we know it is not right for so much of hope, joy, and peace to be stolen from us every day. Yet sometimes there seems to be no escape for us from the treadmill of our daily lives.

We ask Thee to help us, to guide us into a finer way of living. Check our impulse to spread ourselves so thin that we are exposed to fear and doubt, to the weariness and impatience that makes our tempers wear thin, that robs us of peace of mind, that makes skies gray when they should be blue, that stifles a song along the corridors of our heart.

May we have:

- The mercy of God to forgive us.

- The strength of God to make us resolute to do His will.

- The grace of God to be kind, tender, and affectionate one to another.

- The patience of God to believe in the ultimate triumph of Thy kingdom on earth.

This we ask in His name in whom all peace resides. Amen.[2]

Now let's turn to God's Word and learn how to keep anxiety from erasing the peace and joy that should punctuate our lives.

A Quick 'n' Dirty Analysis of Anxiety

Before we meet Christ at the crossroad of our study, let's do a little homework in the Scriptures and gain a basic understanding of this troublesome feeling.

What It Is

Our first clue is found in Philippians 4.

Be anxious for nothing, but in everything by prayer and supplication with thanksgiving let your requests

2. Catherine Marshall, ed., *The Prayers of Peter Marshall* (New York, N.Y.: McGraw-Hill Book Co., 1954), p. 36.

be made known to God. And the peace of God, which surpasses all comprehension, shall guard your hearts and your minds in Christ Jesus. (vv. 6–7)

The word *anxious* in verse 6 comes from the Greek verb *merimnaō*, meaning "to be divided or distracted." In Latin, the same word is translated *anxius*, but with the added shading of choking or strangling. This same menacing nuance also found its way into the German language as *wurgen*, from which we get our word *worry*. So even from ancient times, we can see that worry's nature hasn't changed. It still strangles, it still chokes out life.[3]

So what exactly is anxiety? It is a painful uneasiness due to an impending fear. It's mental, emotional, and spiritual strangulation. At its mildest, we churn inside; at its worst, we panic!

What It Does

First, anxiety highlights the human viewpoint and strangles the divine, so we become fearful. Second, it chokes our ability to distinguish the incidental from the essential, so we get distracted. Third, it twists so many worries around our hearts that we cannot relax, so we become unfruitful. And, fourth, it siphons our energy and joy, making us judgmental rather than accepting, so we become negative.

Enough textbook analysis. Now let's examine it in real life.

A First-Century Portrayal of the Problem

Life doesn't get any more real than in the home. And that's where Luke takes us in one of the most personal and intimate vignettes from Scripture.

The Setting and the People

Now as they were traveling along, He entered a certain village; and a woman named Martha welcomed Him into her home. (Luke 10:38)

Two miles from Jerusalem, in a village called Bethany, Jesus paused at the home of Martha, Mary, and Lazarus. There He knew

---

3. Even Jesus described worry this way, as seen in His illustration of the third soil in His parable of the sower and the seed: "And others are the ones on whom seed was sown among the thorns; these are the ones who have heard the word, and the worries of the world, and the deceitfulness of riches, and the desires for other things enter in and choke the word, and it becomes unfruitful" (Mark 4:18–19).

He would find a refuge among special friends who didn't demand miracles or ask leading questions. It was a home where He knew He was loved and accepted, a place where He knew He could rest.

In *Intimate Moments with the Savior,* author Ken Gire takes us inside the door with Jesus and introduces the two sisters.

> Martha, so eager to serve. Energetic. First to roll up her sleeves and pitch in to help. Last to leave until every dish is cleaned and put away. Up early. First at the market. Haggles to get the best prices. To the point, sometimes even abrupt. The yolks of the eggs she serves for breakfast are never broken. The fruit she sets out in a wooden bowl on the table is always fresh and sweet. Dinner is never overcooked. The perfect hostess.
>
> And Mary? Well, she's up about thirty minutes later. Sometimes goes with her sister to the market, but more often than not, doesn't. The haggling bothers her. Likes to cook, but doesn't like to clean up the mess. Perceptive. Asks few but thoughtful questions. Is a good listener. Sensitive and calm.[4]

Both sisters were delighted to see Jesus. How they expressed their enthusiasm, however, was very different.

The Buildup and the Blowup

Luke first tells us about Mary.

> And she had a sister called Mary, who moreover was listening to the Lord's word, seated at His feet. (v. 39)

Mary was focused; she cleared her mind of all the incidentals and made room for the essential—Jesus. She was content to listen, to be with Christ and not "do" anything. And Martha?

> But Martha was distracted with all her preparations. (v. 40a)

From the moment Christ came in the door, Martha was distracted with all the incidentals of being the perfect hostess. She

---

4. Ken Gire, *Intimate Moments with the Savior* (Grand Rapids, Mich.: Zondervan Publishing House, 1989), p. 64. This book is must reading, especially for those needing help to pause at the Savior's feet.

was busy—too busy. And it wasn't long before those incidentals began grating on her. Take a good look at Martha working in her kitchen, where more than just the oven is heating up.

> *I can't believe Mary isn't in here helping,* she thinks. Martha pushes a fist into the dough. *She should be in here.* Another fist into the dough. *We could get this done in half the time.* She pulls and mashes, pulls and mashes. *You know, I'd like to hear what he has to say, too, but somebody's got to fix dinner.* Martha reaches for some flour and flings it on the lump. *They could at least come in here while they talk.* She works the flour into the expanding loaf. *I can't believe he just lets her sit there.* Another fist into the dough. *Here I am in the kitchen, sweating, working my fingers to the bone . . . doesn't he care?*[5]

Martha was hot, and she kept getting hotter until her anger exploded and she came boiling out of the kitchen, red-faced and frazzled.

> "Lord, do You not care that my sister has left me to do all the serving alone? Then tell her to help me." (v. 40b)

The Scriptures don't say, but you can almost see Martha glaring at Mary the whole time she's chewing out Christ. She's mad at them both, a perfect example of anxiety's results. She's focused on herself, confused about what's incidental and what's essential, unable to relax, and boy, is she judgmental.

The Response and Solution

Jesus' first words after being bawled out were tender ones, "Martha, Martha" (v. 41). You wonder if He didn't stand up and take her into His arms to calm her, much like a father would an exasperated child.

> "You are worried and bothered about so many things." (v. 41)

Jesus understood Martha. He saw beyond the momentary tension and embarrassment and gently addressed the real problem. He

5. Gire, *Intimate Moments*, p. 66.

wasn't to blame, nor was Mary. And all the preparations weren't necessarily the problem either. The problem rested within Martha. It was her attitude. Worry, *merimnaō*, was pulling her apart; she was being strangled by *anxius* and *wurgen*; she was "bothered," which referred to all the outward manifestations of her inner struggle: the disheveled hair, the fiery eyes, the clenched teeth; or maybe, it was the lump of dough she shook in everyone's face. "Oh Martha, Martha,

> . . . only a few things are necessary, really only one,
> for Mary has chosen the good part, which shall not
> be taken away from her." (v. 42)

Anxiety robbed Martha of the essential—fellowship with Christ. She forgot to pause, to insert a comma. Jesus was right there, the Son of God was sitting in her living room, and she chose instead to bake bread, set the table, prepareprepareprepare. Incredible, isn't it? Not really. The last time you felt anxious, did you pause to sit at the Savior's feet? Or did you step over and around Him, distracted with your own preparations?

An Up-Close-and-Personal Examination of Our Exasperation

We get like Martha at times: worried, distracted, all hot and bothered. So what can we do? Here's a little simple arithmetic to help you figure out how to avoid letting life's preparations keep you from joining Mary at the Savior's feet.

We worry when we *add* more things to an already full schedule, when we add pressure by thinking that our worth is determined by our preparations, or when we add expectations to what hasn't even happened yet. Adding makes us angry.

We worry when we *subtract* God's presence from our crisis, or prayer from our day, or perspective from the moment of difficulty. Subtracting makes us doubt.

We worry when we *multiply* our problems by inserting our own solutions too rapidly, looking for a way out instead of His way through. Or when we multiply our fears with our imagination, "What if . . . but maybe . . . ." Multiplying makes us afraid.

We worry when we *divide* life into secular and sacred, when we divide our day into, "This is the Lord's part" and, "This is my own business." Dividing makes us forget.

If you're feeling a bit like Martha, pause once more and offer up this final prayer. The ending has been left open for you to finish with your own words.

25

Dear Savior at whose feet I now sit,

When you knock on the door to my heart, what
is it you are looking for? What is it you want? Is it not
to come in to dine with me? Is it not for fellowship?

And yet, so often, where do you find me? At
your feet? No. In the kitchen. How many times
have I become distracted and left you there . . . sitting . . . waiting . . . longing?

What is so important about my kitchenful of
preparations that draws me away from you? How can
they seem so trivial now and yet so urgent when I'm
caught up in them?

Forgive me for being so much distracted by my
preparations and so little attracted by your presence.
For being so diligent in my duties and so negligent
in my devotion. For being so quick to my feet and
so slow to yours.

Help me to understand that it is an intimate
moment you seek from me, not an elaborate meal.

Guard my heart this day from the many distrac-
tions that vie for my attention. And help me to fix
my eyes on you. Not on my rank in the kingdom,
as did the disciples. Not on the finer points of theology, as did the scribes. Not on the sins of others,
as did the Pharisees. Not on a place of worship, as
did the woman at the well. Not on the budget, as
did Judas. But on you.

Bring me out of the kitchen, Lord. Bid me come
to your feet. And there may I thrill to sit and adore
you. . . .[6]

 Living Insights   STUDY ONE

Some of our hearts are about as calm and peaceful as the floor
of the New York Stock Exchange. Inside there's a feeling of panic.
Worry has flooded the market, causing the value of the fruits of the
Spirit to plummet. Peace is down a thousand points and steadily

6. Gire, *Intimate Moments*, p. 69.

dropping. Joy has posted a disastrous decline. The trading is chaotic and confused. It could be a repeat of the crash of '29 that started the Great Depression.

Is this you? Is there a growing sense of panic in the pit of your stomach? Are you feeling distracted and overwhelmed by worry? Depression could be next—but it doesn't have to be. You can turn the market around with a little sound investing.

Invest your time wisely now by taking stock of the worries that are currently bullish in your life. Personalize the four categories from the lesson to help break them down, being as specific as you can.

I worry when I add _____

_____

I worry when I subtract _____

_____

I worry when I multiply _____

_____

I worry when I divide _____

_____

 Living Insights _____ STUDY TWO

Unlike real stocks and commodities, we can't buy peace or sell anxiety. So what do we do? How can we divest ourselves of worry? One senior advisor in the Christian faith offers this counsel.

> Be anxious for nothing, but in everything by prayer
> and supplication with thanksgiving let your requests
> be made known to God. And the peace of God,
> which surpasses all comprehension, shall guard your
> hearts and your minds in Christ Jesus. (Phil. 4:6–7)

If you're serious about dumping worry and regaining a solid share of God's peace, then stop right now and do exactly what Paul says. Take your portfolio of worries from the previous Living Insight and use it to write your own prayer based on Paul's instructions. Now don't diddle with it or worry about how it will sound, just be as honest and open as you can.

Personal Prayer

_____

_____

_____

_____

_____

_____

_____

_____

_____

_____

_____

_____

_____

_____

_____

_____

Congratulations, you've made a sound investment. One that God promises will pay good dividends. Each time anxiety knocks, just keep investing in prayers like this.[7]

7. For a good tip on how to protect your investment in peace, read Philippians 4:8.

Chapter 4

CHRIST AT THE CROSSROAD OF SHAME
John 8:2–11

Jesus never did anything He needed to be ashamed of. Yet that didn't protect Him against feeling shame—our shame. Do you remember what it cost Him to reconcile us to God?

> God was in Christ reconciling the world to Himself, not counting their trespasses against them. . . . *He made Him who knew no sin to be sin on our behalf,* that we might become the righteousness of God in Him. (2 Cor. 5:19, 21, emphasis added)

The holy and perfect One, the utterly sinless One, took our sins on Himself. Every wicked act committed, all of the darkest thoughts and actions, were fully felt by Him. Auschwitz' horror was there, Stalin's gulags, Cambodia's killing fields, abortion, perversion, selfishness, violence, greed, hate—every disgusting and disobedient sin. We struggle just to deal with the shame of our own sins. But He endured *everyone*'s, for all time, at the same time.

The shame we try to run from, He would not. Instead, He chose the cross, where He took our guilt and shame—not to heap guilt and shame on us—to redeem and release us. His forgiving grace reaches into one of our darkest and most despairing crossroads— the crossroad of shame.

Do you need His strong hand of love to lift you from shame's depths? Then read on to learn the truth about shame and the saving power of Jesus' mercy.

Shame: An Agony All Its Own

What exactly is shame? Webster defines it as "a painful emotion caused by consciousness of guilt, shortcoming, or impropriety . . . a condition of humiliating disgrace or disrepute."[1] Sometimes shame is appropriate, signaling a need to repent and make things right when we have sinned. However, shame can go beyond its

---

1. *Merriam-Webster's Collegiate Dictionary*, 10th ed., see "shame."

proper scope and can batter us into feeling utterly worthless and hopeless, putting us into a state of excruciating despair. Lewis Smedes distills the essence of shame in a quote he uses to open his chapter: "A pervasive sense of shame is the ongoing premise that one is fundamentally bad, inadequate, defective, unworthy, or not fully valid as a human being."[2]

Beyond guilt over what we do, shame persists to attack who we are. Shame goes beyond remorse, is more painful than defeat, is far deeper than disappointment, and is more penetrating than embarrassment. At its worst, it can lead to the most intense form of self-hatred. And when we cannot escape it, when our every thought is stained with self-reproach, we experience a living death—which explains why suicide frequently follows extreme shame. Judas, for example, after he betrayed Jesus, felt an inescapable, irreparable remorse that devolved into agonizing shame. And rather than seeking God's forgiveness, he hanged himself (see Matt. 27:1–5).

But despair need not be the end result of shame. With Christ's transforming grace, we can be rescued from it to begin anew, with our dignity and worth intact. Let's join our Savior now, as He defends and restores a woman caught in the most shameful of circumstances.

An Adulteress and Her Accusers

Another person who experienced extreme shame was the woman caught in adultery. She could not escape the literal nakedness of her guilt, dishonor, and disgrace. And she would have died, too, had she not encountered Christ at her crossroad of shame. Let's revisit that painful juncture in John 8.

> And early in the morning He came again into the
> temple, and all the people were coming to Him; and
> He sat down and began to teach them. (v. 2)

Dawn stole over Jerusalem's temple, and with it came hordes of inquirers. People were attracted to Jesus like bees to honey. Up streets, down stairs, around corners, early risers swarmed through the brisk morning air to gather more of Christ's nectared teachings. Shhhh, He's taking His seat now to teach. The room quiets, there are a few coughs, a sneeze, and once again the sweet words of eternal life flow.

2. Merle Fossum, as quoted by Lewis B. Smedes, in *Shame and Grace: Healing the Shame We Don't Deserve* (San Francisco, Calif.: HarperSanFrancisco, 1993), p. 3.

The calm of that peaceful setting is shattered, however, by a handful of men with hearts honed on hate.

> And the scribes and the Pharisees brought a woman
> caught in adultery. (v. 3)

Christ's words suddenly dry up as the self-righteous intruders put shame on display. Around the room you can hear gasps, feel the mood sour into something ominous as all eyes fasten on the lone figure dumped before Christ.

Her arms bear the marks of a struggle. Her hair is disheveled and there is an audible panic in her breathing. She stands there pulling, clutching at the little she has on, but there isn't enough to protect her from the humiliating stares or to cover the crimson shame on her face. A raised hand with a rock in it silences the stunned onlookers, and a spokesman for the scribes and Pharisees sanctimoniously exposes the woman's sin with titillating detail.

> "Teacher, this woman has been caught in adultery,
> in the very act." (v. 4)

In Greek, the word *caught* used here means "to seize or to overcome." It suggests, according to the tense used and the syntax of the sentence, that the scribes and Pharisees actually pulled the woman from her partner.

And where is the man, her lover? His absence is just as conspicuous as her presence. Has he escaped? It's not likely, since the scribes and Pharisees outnumbered him. It's more likely that he was deliberately allowed to go free. In fact, as you read the account and scrutinize the implications, it's most likely the male partner is one of the accusers, put up to the immoral act beforehand. Why? They just needed the woman as bait for bigger game—Jesus, whom the scribes and Pharisees believe they can bag with a loaded question.

> "Now in the Law Moses commanded us to stone
> such women; what then do You say?" And they were
> saying this, testing Him, in order that they might
> have grounds for accusing Him. (vv. 5–6a)

What grounds? Commentator William Barclay reveals the lethal horns of the dilemma on which the scribes and Pharisees sought to impale Christ.

> If he said that the woman ought to be stoned to
> death, two things followed. First, he would lose the

31

name he had gained for love and for mercy and never again would be called the friend of sinners. Second, he would come into collision with the Roman law, for the Jews had no power to pass or carry out the death sentence on anyone. If he said that the woman should be pardoned, it could immediately be said that He was teaching men to break the law of Moses, and that he was condoning and even encouraging people to commit adultery. That was the trap in which the scribes and Pharisees sought to entrap Jesus.[3]

Justice or mercy? Either way was a snare. The Pharisees have Jesus cornered, or so they think. Instead of answering, however, Christ does something not recorded anywhere else in Scripture.

But Jesus stooped down, and with His finger wrote on the ground. (v. 6b)

What did He write? Some say that Jesus simply doodled in the dust while He collected His thoughts. But the Greek term for *wrote* suggests something more.

The Armenian [translation of the New Testament] translates the passage this way: "He himself, bowing his head, was writing with his finger on the earth to declare their sins; and they were seeing their several sins on the stones." The suggestion is that Jesus was writing in the dust the sins of the very men who were accusing the woman. There may be something in that. The normal Greek word for to *write* is *graphein*; but here the word used is *katagraphein*, which can mean *to write down a record against someone*. . . . It may be that Jesus was confronting those self-confident sadists with the record of their own sins.[4]

Jesus' writing drives the religious wolves into a greater frenzy: "They persisted in asking Him" (v. 7a). The scribes and Pharisees smell blood and are determined to hound their prey into an indefensible position.

3. William Barclay, *The Gospel of John*, vol. 2, rev. ed., The Daily Study Bible Series (Philadelphia, Pa.: Westminster Press, 1975), p. 2.

4. Barclay, *The Gospel of John*, p. 3.

Her Advocate and His Approach

Little did these carnivorous hypocrites realize that, instead of a weak and confused quarry, they were dealing with the Lion of Judah. One reply and He scatters the whole pack.

> He straightened up, and said to them, "He who is without sin among you, let him be the first to throw a stone at her." And again He stooped down, and wrote on the ground. (vv. 7b–8)

Literally, Jesus said, "The sinless one of you, first, on her, let him cast a stone." Though it may sound awkward in English, it carried a tremendous impact in Greek. Enough so that it stunned the scribes and Pharisees into silence. "The sinless one of you, first." Who'll throw the first rock? Step on up, but before you do, be sure your own heart is pure. Tell everyone in this room how it is that you've never committed adultery in your heart. No one could. No one dared.

> And when they heard it, they began to go out one by one, beginning with the older ones, and He was left alone, and the woman, where she had been, in the midst. (v. 9)

Peter Marshall saw the scene this way:

> Looking into their faces, Christ sees into the yesterdays that lie deep in the pools of memory and conscience. He sees into their very hearts, and that moving finger writes on . . .
> > Idolater . . .
> > Liar . . .
> > Drunkard . . .
> > Murderer . . .
> > Adulterer . . .
> There is the thud of stone after stone falling on the pavement.
> Not many of the Pharisees are left.
> One by one, they creep away—like animals—slinking into the shadows . . .
> > shuffling off into the crowded streets to lose themselves in the multitudes.[5]

5. Peter Marshall, in A Man Called Peter, by Catherine Marshall (New York, N.Y.: Avon Books, 1951), p. 323.

Though her accusers leave, the guilt of this woman's sin still remains, shame still burns inside her in a smoldering self-hate. So what if no one condemned her? She condemns herself.

But Jesus doesn't.

> And straightening up, Jesus said to her, "Woman, where are they? Did no one condemn you?" And she said, "No one, Lord." And Jesus said, "Neither do I condemn you; go your way. From now on sin no more." (vv. 10–11)

The only one qualified to condemn this woman didn't. The only one powerful enough to set her free from shame did. With honesty—"Go and sin no more," and compassion—"Neither do I condemn you," Jesus gently removes her guilt and shame and clothes her with His righteousness and love. He sets her free! And He can do the same for you.

To All Weighed Down by Shame

There are moments in all our lives when we get "caught in the very act." It may not be adultery, but it's sin just the same. And like that woman, we, too, will be accosted by rock throwers who are not qualified to condemn, but do. People who will take a sordid delight in publicizing our shame.

For your own sake, stay away from Pharisees like that. Don't allow them to use you for target practice. Instead, draw near and confess your sin to the One who is qualified to condemn, but doesn't—Jesus. In Romans, the apostle Paul declares,

> There is therefore now no condemnation for those who are in Christ Jesus. (8:1)

Even if it had been you instead of that woman who was dragged before Christ that morning, His words would have been and still are the same, "Neither do I condemn you; go your way. From now on sin no more." You're free!

 Living Insights

Oftentimes, not even our intimate friends know about our deepest feelings of shame. The shameful thing that we did or that was done to us seems too horrible to tell, too grotesque. It makes us feel worthless and ugly just to think about it, so we try not to. We push away those painful memories that awaken our shame—denying them, locking them in the closet, doing anything to smother the accusing voice inside us that sneers, "Tramp! Stupid! Pervert! You deserve to suffer."

Shame is a powerful emotion. Powerful enough to twist our lives into a living hell. Powerful enough to even drive some to suicide. But suicide is not the way to silence our shame—and neither is denial.

What will silence it, then? We could do the one thing that we always, absolutely, feel would be the worst thing to do: We could expose the raw disgrace of our shame voluntarily. We could walk into the temple, instead of being dragged, and ask Jesus to free us as He did the woman caught in adultery.

Would you be willing to confide your shame in Jesus? You've seen how He dealt with the adulteress. He's already paid the penalty for your sin, experienced your shame on the Cross. Nothing you have done or said or even thought will surprise Him. And He promises not to reject you:

> "The one who comes to Me I will certainly not cast out." (John 6:37b)

Because of the sensitive nature of what we're dealing with, if you are willing to confess, to confide in the Lord Jesus, then simply write only a word or phrase that represents one particular situation. Do it now. Step inside the temple and tell Him, "Lord, I have been caught in _____, in the very act," or, "Lord, I was victimized; because of _____, I feel a deep sense of shame." Take whatever time is necessary and get it all out, as you pour out your heart to the Lord in prayer.

Now let Jesus respond. For as long as you can, just sit and listen, allow Him to speak to you through His Word and release you from your guilt and shame.

◆

> "Come to Me, all who are weary and heavy-laden, and I will give you rest. Take My yoke upon you, and learn from Me, for I am gentle and humble in heart; and you shall find rest for your souls." (Matt. 11:28–29)

◆

The truth is that no condemnation now hangs over the head of those who are "in" Christ Jesus. For the new spiritual principle of life "in" Christ Jesus lifts me out of the old vicious circle of sin and death. (Rom. 8:1–2 PHILLIPS)

◆

Who will bring a charge against God's elect? God is the one who justifies; who is the one who condemns? Christ Jesus is He who died, yes, rather who was raised, who is at the right hand of God, who also intercedes for us. Who shall separate us from the love of Christ? Shall tribulation, or distress, or persecution, or famine, or nakedness, or peril, or sword? . . . For I am convinced that neither death, nor life, nor angels, nor principalities, nor things present, nor things to come, nor powers, nor height, nor depth, nor any other created thing, shall be able to separate us from the love of God, which is in Christ Jesus our Lord. (Rom. 8:33–35, 38–39)

◆

"Neither do I condemn you; go your way. From now on sin no more." (John 8:11b; see also Ps. 103:10–14)

"No condemnation? You mean I don't have to beat myself up anymore over the past?" No. Jesus doesn't. It's over. Cling to your forgiveness in Him, not your shame. You're free!

 ## Living Insights

Even now, as some of you read this Living Insight, you will still *feel* bound to shame despite what you confessed. And so you wonder, "Did I not pray sincerely enough? Use the right words? What?"

Don't lose hope. Yes, you are forgiven, but you have to understand that biblical truth is not a magic wand. We cannot wave a few promises over our heads and expect all the feelings of shame in our hearts to suddenly disappear. They're still there. And the only way to get rid of them is to consciously, diligently, weed them out with the truth. Romans 12:2 states:

Do not be conformed to this world, but be transformed by the renewing of your mind, that you may prove what the will of God is, that which is good and acceptable and perfect.

Renewing your mind—that's what you started doing in Study One. Renewing your mind to the liberating truth that "there is therefore now no condemnation for those who are in Christ Jesus" (Rom. 8:1). Now hold on to that truth. Plant it, water it, let it sink its roots deep into your thinking. When you catch yourself starting to feel shame over something you've already confessed to Christ, stop! Focus instead on Christ's compassion and forgiveness. Renew your thinking right then and there based on God's Word.

Paul touched on this same process in his letter to the Ephesians.

> In reference to your former manner of life, you lay aside the old self, which is being corrupted in accordance with the lusts of deceit, and that you be renewed in the spirit of your mind, and put on the new self, which in the likeness of God has been created in righteousness and holiness of the truth. (4:22–24)

Shame isn't easy to weed out, especially when it has already been spreading its roots in our hearts for years. Don't get discouraged; just keep cultivating the truth. And as Jesus promised, "If you abide in My word, then you are truly disciples of Mine; and you shall know the truth, and the truth shall make you free" (John 8:31b–32).

Chapter 5

CHRIST AT THE CROSSROAD OF AMBITION

Mark 10:35–45

By the pricking of my thumbs,
Something wicked this way comes.
Open, locks,
Whoever knocks!

Enter Macbeth.[1]

Ambition came to Shakespeare's Macbeth on a desolate heath beneath a grumbling sky soiled with foul and foggy air. Not exactly where he expected to find it, but there it was, or actually, there they were: the witches three whose prophesy foretold who the king of Scotland next would be—Macbeth!

Do you remember the first bewitching stanza of the witches' recipe for reckless ambition?

Double, double, toil and trouble;
Fire burn and cauldron bubble.
Fillet of a fenny snake,
In the cauldron boil and bake;
Eye of newt and toe of frog,
Wool of bat and tongue of dog,
Adder's fork and blind-worm's sting,
Lizard's leg and howlet's wing,
For a charm of powerful trouble,
Like a hell-broth boil and bubble.[2]

That charm of powerful trouble boils and bubbles a murderous desire in Macbeth's heart for Scotland's imperial crown. The alchemy of greed, deceit, and vaulting ambition transforms his life

---

1. William Shakespeare, *Macbeth*, in *The Plays and Sonnets of William Shakespeare*, ed. William George Clarke and William Aldis Wright (Chicago, Ill.: Encyclopaedia Britannica, 1952), vol. 2, p. 300.

2. Shakespeare, *Macbeth*, p. 300.

into a hell-broth of sedition. He gains the crown, but forfeits his soul (Mark 8:36). The Lady Macbeth forfeits hers as well; a blood-guilty complicity drives her to madness and suicide. And in bitter repose, Macbeth denounces life and the vanity of ambition.

> Out, out, brief candle!
> Life's but a walking shadow, a poor player
> That struts and frets his hour upon the stage
> And then is heard no more. It is a tale
> Told by an idiot, full of sound and fury,
> Signifying nothing.[3]

The Dark Side of Ambition

"Fair is foul, and foul is fair,"[4] the witches wail in the opening scene of that Shakespearean tragedy; and there is no better definition of the twisted ethics behind ruthless ambition. It shares no Golden Rule with the rest of us. It has no sympathy or other praiseworthy feelings. It only concerns itself with results, achievement, power. Nothing else matters.

Does this mean that being motivated to do a job well or to dream dreams is wrong? No. The Scriptures are replete with exhortations to be steadfast and immovable in our pursuit of excellence. The goal of excellence can, however, subtly become a lust for accomplishment if driven by the sin of pride.

What Ambition Means—according to Webster

According to Webster, ambition is "an ardent desire for rank, fame, power . . . strong desire for advancement."[5] Me, me, me. That's the dark side—everything centered on self, how it affects me, how I will benefit.

How Ambition Works—according to Solomon

Solomon paints several stark portraits of how ambition really works, portraits that are strikingly different from the world's glossy depiction. Study them carefully, for it's when we forsake their messages that our focus shifts to self-advancement.

---

3. Shakespeare, *Macbeth*, p. 309.

4. Shakespeare, *Macbeth*, p. 284.

5. *Webster's Ninth New Collegiate Dictionary*, see "ambition."

> Before destruction the heart of man is haughty,
> But humility goes before honor. (Prov. 18:12)

> A man's pride will bring him low,
> But a humble spirit will obtain honor. (29:23)

> A greedy man brings trouble to his family,
> but he who hates bribes will live (15:27 NIV)

> It is not good to eat much honey,
> Nor is it glory to search out one's own glory. (25:27)[6]

Over in the New Testament we have another portrait of this "charm of powerful trouble." Let's turn there now, to Mark 10, where the drama unfolds.

> By the pricking of my thumbs,
> Something wicked this way comes.
>> Open, locks,
>> Whoever knocks!

> *Enter* The ambitious sons of Zebedee.

Jesus' Response to Ambition

The backdrop to the scene we're about to witness is important for us to picture. Jesus is on the road to Jerusalem with His disciples; soon the crowds will be heaping palm branches and praises before Him. But Jesus' thoughts aren't taken up with His own popularity. He knows that soon enough this same gentle crowd will become an angry mob shrieking, "Crucify Him!" He thinks, instead, about humbling Himself to the point of death on a cross, about His triumphant resurrection, and about His beloved disciples. Suddenly He stops, pulls the Twelve aside, and tells them the events to come in graphic detail (Mark 10:32–34). He will be condemned to death, mocked, spit upon, scourged, killed; then He will rise again—this is the future Jesus tries to prepare them for.

But James and John are interested only in the future advancement of their own power and glory.

Dialogue

> And James and John, the two sons of Zebedee, came up to Him, saying to Him, "Teacher, we want

6. For further study, see Proverbs 15:32–33; 23:4–5; 27:2; 29:23, 25.

You to do for us whatever we ask of You." (v. 35)

You cannot help but shake your head in wonder at the brothers' brashness. The selfish naiveté of such a request is colossal. You'd almost think these were children speaking to the Master, not grown men. But like a wise father, Jesus doesn't immediately give an answer to such an open-ended question. Instead, He draws out the raw ambition behind James and John's request.

> And He said to them, "What do you want Me to do for you?" And they said to Him, "Grant that we may sit in Your glory, one on Your right, and one on Your left." (vv. 36–37)

The sons of Zebedee are positioning themselves for power. They want greatness. They want to have a position of influence higher than any of the other disciples when Jesus establishes His kingdom in Jerusalem. But Jesus isn't going to that city to rule from a throne, but from a cross. And so He tells them:

> "You do not know what you are asking for. Are you able to drink the cup that I drink, or to be baptized with the baptism with which I am baptized?" (v. 38)

"The cup" and "the baptism" are both symbolic references to the suffering that lay ahead for Jesus. "Are you prepared to earn the glory you seek by first suffering shame, anguish—even death?" And they answered, "We are able" (v. 39a). The presumption in the brothers' flippant reply is incredible. "You bet, no problem. Count us in. We can handle it." Yet not many days later, in the Garden of Gethsemane, James and John quickly decided that being on either side of Jesus wasn't such a good idea after all, and they ran.

Looking ahead, Jesus assures these boastful brothers that they will suffer for His sake, even to death.

> And Jesus said to them, "The cup that I drink you shall drink; and you shall be baptized with the baptism with which I am baptized." (v. 39b)

For James, that meant being the first apostle to be martyred (Acts 12:2). And as for his brother John, it meant being the last apostle to die after years of persecution and exile.

Even so, Christ explains that He cannot reserve them special seats in heaven.

"But to sit on My right or on My left, this is not Mine to give; but it is for those for whom it has been prepared." (Mark 10:40)

Being promoted to a place of authority in God's kingdom is not a matter of knowing the right person or pulling the right strings. Prominence comes by appointment only, and God alone is the One who "puts down one, and exalts another" (see Ps. 75:5–7).

As you might suspect, the other disciples figured out what James and John were up to, and their blood began to boil and bubble.

And hearing this, the ten began to feel indignant with James and John. (Mark 10:41)

In Greek, the word for *indignant* used here means "to grieve much; annoyance, vexation."[7] Peter, Matthew, Judas, all of them were irritated. Why? Read what happened only a short time earlier.

And they came to Capernaum; and when He was in the house, He began to question them, "What were you discussing on the way?" But they kept silent, for on the way they had discussed with one another which of them was the greatest. (9:33–34)

They had all envisioned themselves reigning with Jesus on either His left or His right. James and John were just the first to have the courage to hit Jesus up about it. And with self-righteous indignation, they all glare at James and John.

Discourse

Jesus senses the toil and trouble brewing between His disciples. And He knows why it's there. This isn't the road to Jerusalem they are on, it is the crossroad of ambition. So He quickly pulls the Twelve aside and gives them instructions on how to achieve greatness His way.

"You know that those who are recognized as rulers of the Gentiles lord it over them; and their great men exercise authority over them." (10:42)

First, Jesus briefly reminds them of the chain of command that exists in the rank and file of everyday life. Every profession has its

7. W. E. Vine, *Vine's Expository Dictionary of New Testament Words* (McLean, Va.: MacDonald Publishing Co., n.d.), p. 58.

leaders; they are there in the military, in politics, in business—it's just the way the system works. For His followers, however, Jesus has a different system in mind.

> "But *it is not so among you,* but whoever wishes to become great among you shall be your servant; and whoever wishes to be first among you shall be slave of all." (vv. 43–44, emphasis added)

In Christ's church, the way up is down. Servanthood is what Jesus desires, not selfish ambition. Greatness comes from serving for the glory of God, not from being served for our own glory. And the best example that ever lived was standing right there in front of them.

> "For even the Son of Man did not come to be served,
> but to serve, and to give His life a ransom for many."
> (v. 45)

With that, Jesus and the disciples once again started walking down the road to Jerusalem, to a cross where servanthood would be demonstrated at its most selfless extreme.

Ways to Hold Ambition in Check

> [Life's] a tale
> Told by an idiot, full of sound and fury,
> Signifying nothing.

Macbeth's rueful words are haunting. They await all those who get caught up in the sound and fury of their own selfish ambitions as he did.

To avoid the specter of a vain and empty life, *remember* the life-style of the kingdom: servanthood (v. 43). *Release* the controls to God. Let Him reward you with the promotions He has prepared for you (v. 40). And last, *return* to the priorities of Christ, to serve and give, not take (v. 45).

> "For what does it profit a man to gain the whole world, and forfeit his soul?" (8:36)

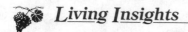

Living Insights

In his insightful book *Spiritual Values in Shakespeare*, Ernest Marshall Howse writes,

> Macbeth is excited because the witches suddenly give form and definition to greed as yet unpurposed. They add fuel to fires already kindled. They bring an idea to a mind prepared to receive it. . . . Shakespeare lets us see that the susceptible disposition meets the tempting opportunity. What life does to you depends upon what life finds in you.[8]

What has life found in you? What have your spouse and employer found in you this last week? A servant's attitude like Christ's? Or perhaps a self-seeking, "I want you to do for me whatever I ask of you" attitude like James and John's?

Let's try something. First, fill in the following spaces with the appropriate name.

(Spouse) _____ ,

_____

(Employer) _____ ,

_____

(Parent) _____ ,

_____

(Child) _____ ,

_____

(Pastor) _____ ,

_____

(Friend) _____ ,

_____

8. Ernest Marshall Howse, *Spiritual Values in Shakespeare* (New York, N.Y.: Abingdon Press, 1955), p. 58.

Now go back and, below each name, fill in the statement that best fits your attitude toward that person. Is it, "What will you do for me?" Or, "What can I do for you?"

Last, looking ahead to next week, in what specific ways could you demonstrate a servant's heart toward any of the people above that you have selfishly demanded serve you?

_____

_____

_____

_____

_____

 Living Insights   STUDY TWO

Are you still a human *being*? Or has ambition transformed you into a human "doing"—driven by accomplishment, driven by deadlines, driven by competition, driven, driven, driven? One way to find out is by examining your heart with the following probing questions.

- Are you all business—intense in every area of your life, viewing rest and quiet as a waste of time?

- Are you always busy?

- Does the end justify the means for you—has integrity become inconvenient?

- Do you find yourself competing with people more than simply being present with them?

- Do you blow up easily, blasting others with outbursts of anger?

What's the diagnosis? Are you infected with an acute case of ambition? Use the space provided to summarize your findings. Be specific. For example, if you feel your integrity has slipped, identify where and in what ways.

_____

_____

_____

_____

_____

_____

_____

Finally, and this may hurt a little, how can you change your condition from a driven "human doing" to a serving human being? Mark 10:35–45 will prescribe a cure.

_____

_____

_____

_____

_____

_____

_____

Chapter 6

CHRIST AT THE CROSSROAD OF DEATH

John 11:1–45

Joseph Bayly knew about death. It was a subject in which he was well tutored.

His teachers were a newborn son who died after surgery, a five-year-old son who died from leukemia, and an eighteen-year-old son who died after a sledding accident complicated by mild hemophilia. Each imparted a painful lesson in the stark reality of death. A reality that Bayly confronts us all with in the opening of his book *The Last Thing We Talk About*.

> The hearse began its grievous journey many thousand years ago, as a litter made of saplings.
>
> Litter, sled, wagon, Cadillac: the conveyance has changed, but the corpse it carries is the same.
>
> Birth and death enclose man in a sort of parenthesis of the present. And the brackets at the beginning and end of life are still impenetrable.
>
> This frustrates us, especially in a time of scientific breakthrough and exploding knowledge, that we should be able to break out of earth's environment and yet be stopped cold by death's unyielding mystery. Electroencephalogram may replace mirror held before the mouth, autopsies may become more sophisticated, cosmetic embalming may take the place of pennies on the eyelids and canvas shrouds, but death continues to confront us with its blank wall. Everything changes; death is changeless. . . .
>
> Dairy farmer and sales executive live in death's shadow, with Nobel prize winner and prostitute, mother, infant, teen, old man. The hearse stands waiting for the surgeon who transplants a heart as well as the hopeful recipient, for the funeral director as well as the corpse he manipulates.

Death spares none.[1]

Sobering words. The kind needed if we're to honestly face death. But not everyone is willing to face it. Many would rather skip class than learn about this subject. And there are plenty who do. Let's briefly look at some of the ways people attempt to avoid this hardest lesson in life's curriculum.

Familiar Reactions to the Subject of Death

Many of us cope with the harshness of death by joking about it. We use humor as a kind of painkiller to anesthetize ourselves against the violence, the loss, and the grief. We try to keep it at arm's length with lighthearted quips.

Others attempt to distance themselves from death by simply not talking about it. Bayly noted,

> We are critical of the Victorians because they senti-
> mentalized death and surrounded it with pathos.
> But modern man denies it. The sort of taboo
> Victorians placed on public discussion of sex has
> been transferred to death in our culture. . . .
> This conspiracy of silence in the twilight of the
> century has produced a denial of death without prece-
> dent in Western civilization.[2]

Still others rely on graceful hymns, fragrant flowers, and the em-balmer's art to make death beautiful. But, as helpful to the living as these may be, none of them can truly mask death's ugly reality.

> Death destroys beauty. . . .
> When the automobile's victim is human, when
> a child not a bird, a man not a mole lies dead on
> the road, we see the true nature of death. . . .
> Beauty destroyed by ten pills, achievement ter-
> minated by a seven-story fall, youth's glory ended by
> a grenade, women and children charred by napalm:
> these are the faces of death.

1. Joseph Bayly, *The Last Thing We Talk About*, rev. ed. (Elgin, Ill.: David C. Cook Publishing Co., 1973), pp. 11–12.
2. Bayly, *Last Thing We Talk About*, p. 18.

Coronary, cancer, stroke, infection. Death comes, even normally, in a multitude of ways, to every human condition, every age.

Shall we deny death and try to make it beautiful?

A corpse is never beautiful, animal corpse or corpse of man. . . .

We cannot beautify death. We may live with it and accept it, but we cannot change its foul nature.[3]

Last, the universal reaction to death is fear. We cannot explain this great mystery, and such a dark unknown makes us afraid. We dread its pain and nothingness. We spend our whole lives struggling futilely against the inexorable pull of that one unchangeable fact— death spares none.

Someday, when either we or someone we love is dying, that brutal truth will no longer be funny or distant or merely a mystery to us. It will be agonizingly real, just as it was to Mary and Martha in the first century when their brother Lazarus died. Let's turn to that scene recorded in John chapter 11.

Death at Bethany: A Story of Grief and Faith

Only a short distance from Jerusalem's bustling streets was a smaller, quieter community named Bethany. There the two sisters and brother lived who, outside of the disciples, may well have been Jesus' closest friends. We met Mary and Martha in our previous lesson on anxiety. Lazarus, possibly the youngest of the three, was their bachelor brother. And according to John 11:1–2, he was sick, very sick.

Sickness Turns to Death

Whatever remedies they tried, nothing worked, and Lazarus quickly deteriorated from just being sick to dying. In desperation, the sisters sent a message to Jesus saying, "Lord, behold, he whom You love is sick" (v. 3). They didn't beg or demand that He come; they didn't need to. When people share a love such as theirs, no invitations are needed (v. 5). But Christ didn't go. Instead, He deliberately tarried for two more days (v. 6).

3. Bayly, *Last Thing We Talk About*, pp. 14–15.

Meanwhile, Mary and Martha kept expecting to see Jesus with each new visitor at their door. "Hang on, Lazarus," they urged, "Jesus is coming. The Master will heal you. Fight it." And he did, all day and night. But by midmorning the next day, the sickness was clearly about to win the battle. A pall of death clung to his flesh. The sisters' hope turned into panic and confusion. "Where is Jesus? What could be taking Him so long?" Martha had done everything she knew to do. She felt exhausted and undone. Mary held her brother's hand. His breathing was ever so slight. "He'll come," she whispered in his ear. But then it was too late. Lazarus died.

When Jesus finally did end His delay, He told the disciples,

> "Let us go to Judea again. . . . Our friend Lazarus
> has fallen asleep; but I go, that I may awaken him
> out of sleep." (vv. 7, 11)

Now this totally baffled the disciples, who thought He was referring to a literal sleep (vv. 12–13). So Jesus put it to them bluntly, "Lazarus is dead" (v. 14).

Delay Leads to Blame

The news of Lazarus' death spread, and friends came from all around to grieve with the sisters and attend the funeral (vv. 17–19). Four days later, Jesus approached the outskirts of the city, and Martha immediately went out to meet Him (v. 20). Only not to embrace Him, but to blame.

> "Lord, if You had been here, my brother would not
> have died." (v. 21)

"Where were you, Lord? If You had come, my brother would still be alive. But You waited, You delayed. *Why*, Lord?" Her voice is raw, edgy. It's a painful moment. The words hurt. Martha loves Jesus, but her disillusionment and grief push her to vent her bitterness. Mary felt the same way. With hot tears, she fell at His feet and poured out the frustrated hope that burned its way into her heart with each day He delayed.

> "Lord, if You had been here, my brother would not
> have died." (v. 32)

Even those who grieved with the sisters grumbled about Jesus' timing. "Could not this man, who opened the eyes of him who was blind, have kept this man also from dying?" (v. 37).

It was a bitter reception at Bethany. Nevertheless, Jesus ached with compassion for His friends. He understood their pain, for He had loved Lazarus too.

> When Jesus therefore saw her weeping, and the Jews who came with her, also weeping, He was deeply moved in spirit, and was troubled, and said, "Where have you laid him?" They said to Him, "Lord, come and see." Jesus wept. (vv. 33–35)

Prayer Results in a Miracle

The mourning continued as Mary and Martha led Jesus to a cave sealed by a great rock—Lazarus' tomb (v. 38). They had come, they thought, so Jesus could pay His last respects to the dead. But Jesus had something else in mind.

Jesus said, "Remove the stone." (v. 39a)

Martha was horrified by the grisly idea.

> "Lord, by this time there will be a stench, for he has been dead four days." Jesus said to her, "Did I not say to you, if you believe, you will see the glory of God?" And so they removed the stone. And Jesus raised His eyes, and said, "Father, I thank Thee that Thou heardest Me. And I knew that Thou hearest Me always; but because of the people standing around I said it, that they may believe that Thou didst send Me." And when He had said these things, He cried out with a loud voice, "Lazarus, come forth." (vv. 39b–43)

Grief Changes to Belief

Everyone looked. Some of them covered their noses to protect against the cave's ghastly breath, but no one's eyes left that dark, gaping maw. Suddenly, Mary gasped, and the bewildered sisters clutched each other more tightly. Something moved. Something alive!

> He who had died came forth, bound hand and foot with wrappings; and his face was wrapped around with a cloth. Jesus said to them, "Unbind him, and let him go." (v. 44)

Lazarus was back! And two weeping, smiling, giggling sisters quickly unwrapped Christ's unexpected gift and were united with their brother again.

Lazarus, however, wasn't the only one raised from the dead that day. There were others; eyewitnesses who, because of what they saw, believed in Jesus and passed from death into life—eternal life.

> Many therefore of the Jews, who had come to
> Mary and beheld what He had done, believed in
> Him. (v. 45; see also 5:24)

And You? What about You?

Jesus raised Lazarus because He promised He would: "Your brother shall rise again" (v. 23). And He also promises to raise all those who believe in Him.

> "I am the resurrection and the life; he who believes
> in Me shall live even if he dies." (v. 25)

Have you passed from death into life through faith in Christ? Romans 6:23 states:

> For the wages of sin is death, but the free gift of God
> is eternal life in Christ Jesus our Lord. (v. 23)

Death spares no one. But it isn't the end. It is simply the transition that takes us from this temporary life to eternal life, believer and nonbeliever alike. The question is, Where will you spend it?

 Living Insights

Two words every Christian needs to remember are *never assume*. Never assume your neighbors are Christians just because they go to church. Never assume that a person is a believer because he or she attends a Bible study. Never assume that people know Jesus simply because they carry a Bible. Why? Because you're cynical? No. Because many people who carry Bibles, attend studies, and go to church don't know Christ. And we blind ourselves to the opportunities of helping them pass from death into life every time we assume.

Suppose you don't assume and you ask that friend at church to share with you when he or she became a Christian. And this person says, "Well, I've been going to church all my life." How would you respond? Does church attendance secure salvation? What does? Could you explain the gospel in twenty-five words or less? Could you accurately quote the relevant Scriptures without using a Bible?

Try writing down the gospel in twenty-five words or less and give Scripture references.

_____

_____

_____

_____

_____

Don't be surprised if you couldn't. Just as we tend to assume that others know Christ, many of us also assume that because we're saved, we know how to explain salvation to others. If you need help in sharing the basics of the gospel, study the following illustration and memorize the key verses.

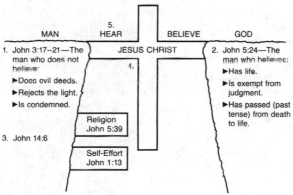

1. Man is separated from God and is under judgment because of sin (John 3:17–21, 36). (See also Romans 3:23, 6:23; Hebrews 9:27.)

2. The many statements made by Jesus about eternal life indicate there is a solution to this separation (John 5:24).

3. Man attempts to build his own bridges (1:13), but Jesus declares Himself to be the only Way (14:6). (See also Ephesians 2:8–9.)

4. Jesus is the Way because of who He is: God (John 1:14); the Lamb (1:36) . . . and because of what He

53

did: He died (6:51; see also Romans 5:8); He rose from the dead (John 11:25).

5. Jesus calls on us to act on this message—to hear and believe (5:24). Synonyms: receive (1:12); be reborn (3:3); drink (4:13). (See also Revelation 3:20.)[4]

By the way, before we leave this Living Insight, exactly when was it that *you* became a Christian? Would you mind sharing? Let's do that in our next study.

 ## Living Insights

STUDY TWO

The Scriptures teach that we should all be ready to give an account of the hope that is in us (1 Pet. 3:15). That's what a personal testimony is all about—telling others how we came to know Jesus. When we stop assuming that others are Christians and start asking, God will provide us with many opportunities for sharing our testimonies. Are you prepared?

On a separate sheet of paper, write out your personal testimony. Try keeping it around five to seven minutes long. If you need help putting it together, use these three guidelines. First, briefly explain what your life was like before you met Christ. Second, tell how you came to believe in Jesus as your Savior. And third, describe how your life has been different since. Once it is written, share it with a close friend to help you evaluate how clear it is and what still needs work.

4. Illustration and quote by Jim Petersen, *Living Proof* (Colorado Springs, Colo.: NavPress, 1989), pp. 248–49. Used by permission.

Chapter 7

CHRIST AT THE CROSSROAD OF DOUBT

John 20:24–29

Opinions about doubt vary—greatly. To some, doubt represents rank unbelief, the worst kind of blasphemy. Martin Luther, for example, felt that he had no greater enemy than doubt. He called it this "monster of uncertainty," a "gospel of despair."[1]

Others, though, argue that it is essential to any intelligent pursuit of the truth. Tennyson wrote,

> There lives more faith in honest doubt,
> Believe me, than in half the creeds.[2]

The church has always had its godly individuals whose perspectives differed greatly, especially on the subject of doubt. But must we choose sides? Isn't it possible for faith and doubt to coexist? There is at least one person who would emphatically say, "Yes!" He is the desperate father who brought his demon-possessed child to Jesus. Just listen to the conflict of despair and hope in his voice.

> "If You can do anything, take pity on us and help us!" And Jesus said to him, " 'If You can!' All things are possible to him who believes." Immediately the boy's father cried out and began saying, "I do believe; help my unbelief." (Mark 9:22b–24)

That is as raw an expression of honest faith and doubt as you'll find anywhere. The father could say nothing less. Since the demon had come, his son had been mute and frequently writhed in convulsions that left him foaming at the mouth like a dying animal. Friends backed away; others hurried past in fright. Life became messy and ugly for them, something no one wanted to see or be associated with. And it was in this tormented soil that the father's

---

1. Ewald M. Plass, comp., *What Luther Says* (Saint Louis, Mo.: Concordia Publishing House, 1959), vol. 1, p. 426.

2. Alfred, Lord Tennyson, from "In Memoriam," in *Masterpieces of Religious Verse*, ed. James Dalton Morrison (New York, N.Y.: Harper and Brothers Publishers, 1948), p. 387.

55

faith struggled to grow. He didn't learn theology listening to educated rabbis from inside a quiet synagogue. His faith developed in the disturbing lessons of pulling a thrashing son out of fires each time the demon tried to destroy him (vv. 17–22).

Disturbing lessons occur in all our lives. Messy ones that send doubts fissuring deep into those sacred beliefs we once thought rock-solid and beyond question. It's in those moments of dark turmoil that we, like that father, cry out, "Lord, I believe; help my unbelief!"

When Doubts Emerge: "I Do Not Understand"

Doubt comes to us when we reach the limits of our understanding. When we encounter a sudden, unexpected calamity. When we pray for a certain thing and the exact opposite occurs. When a respected mentor suddenly denies the faith and walks away. When we obey and do what is right and suffer miserably for it. When we take a course at school that seems to make more sense than the faith we have been raised in. When life takes us through twists and turns that make absolutely no sense. These are the kinds of circumstances that often raise unsettling questions. But should we be afraid of those questions? Run from them? No.

> Questions . . . are the grappling hooks by which the sheer summits of truth can be scaled.
>
> Consequently, those hooks, however sharp, should not be feared. Neither should they be discouraged. For questions are the very hooks by which a person climbs from doubt to faith.[3]

People who honestly face the questions raised by their doubts are what Daniel Taylor calls "reflective Christians." In his book *The Myth of Certainty,* he writes:

> The reflective person is, first and foremost, a question asker—one who finds in every experience and assertion something that requires further investigation. He or she is a stone-turner, attracted to the creepy-crawly things that live under rocks and behind human pronouncements. The writer of

3. From the study guide *Issues and Answers in Jesus' Day,* coauthored by Ken Gire, from the Bible-teaching ministry of Charles R. Swindoll (Fullerton, Calif.: Insight for Living, 1990), p. 2.

Ecclesiastes was such a person: "I directed my mind to know, to investigate, and to seek wisdom and an explanation . . ." (Eccles. 7:25).[4]

Are you a stone-turner? Jesus had a disciple who definitely was. His name was Didymus—more commonly known as Doubting Thomas. But that really isn't a fair nickname. "Reflective Thomas" is more appropriate. Why? Let's turn over a few rocks in the Scriptures and find out.

Why Thomas Struggled: "I Will Not Believe"

Thomas was a thinker. He had the courage to question, to admit the struggles, to raise his hand and say, "Wait, I don't understand. None of this is making sense to me." He even had the courage to die, as we'll see in John 11.

You'll remember from our last lesson that, two days after hearing of Lazarus' illness, Jesus announced to His disciples, "Let us go to Judea again" (v. 7). The Twelve knew this trip would be dangerous and immediately tried to dissuade Him.

"Rabbi, the Jews were just now seeking to stone You,
and are You going there again?" (v. 8)

Roughly translated, the disciples were saying, "Lord, are you crazy? That's asking to be killed!"

At that moment the disciples might well have refused to follow Jesus. . . . They were all feeling that to go to Jerusalem was to go to their deaths, and they were hanging back.[5]

Just then Thomas offered an earnest proposal that revealed an important aspect of his character.

Thomas therefore, who is called Didymus, said to his fellow disciples, "Let us also go, that we may die with Him." (v. 16)

Thomas said *that*? The same Thomas whose nickname causes everybody to snicker? Yes. The truth is, he was a man of great

4. Daniel Taylor, *The Myth of Certainty* (Waco, Tex.: Word Books, Jarrell, 1986), p. 16.

5. William Barclay, *The Gospel of John*, vol. 2, rev. ed., The Daily Study Bible Series (Philadelphia, Pa.: Westminster Press, 1975), p. 87.

courage. Remember, this wasn't an idle boast from someone who knew Lazarus was going to be raised from the dead. Thomas honestly believed he would be returning to Judea to die. But he was determined to stand by Jesus no matter what the cost.[6]

Another glimpse of Thomas' struggle with faith and doubt is revealed at the Last Supper (John 13–14). The disciples' stomachs had churned through practically the whole meal. They were upset, not by the bitter herbs they ate, but by the bitter words doled out for them to digest. Words like, "One of you will betray Me," and, "Where I go, you cannot follow Me now." Then, too, Christ's comments about everyone knowing their way to His Father's house didn't settle well either.

> "Let not your heart be troubled; believe in God, believe also in Me. In My Father's house are many dwelling places; if it were not so, I would have told you; for I go to prepare a place for you. And if I go and prepare a place for you, I will come again, and receive you to Myself; that where I am, there you may be also. And you know the way where I am going." Thomas said to Him, "Lord, we do not know where You are going, how do we know the way?" (14:1–5)

Only Thomas had the courage to question. He could have sat there quietly with the rest of the disciples, but it would have gone totally against his nature to pretend he understood when he didn't. And we can be glad he did ask his question, because it prompted Jesus to give the clearest directions to the Father's house in all of Scripture.

> Jesus said to him, "I am the way, and the truth, and the life; no one comes to the Father, but through Me." (v. 6)

Perhaps now we can appreciate more deeply than ever this reflective disciple's struggle to believe at his crossroad of doubt found in John 20.

After Jesus' arrest and crucifixion, every creepy-crawly doubt imaginable was uncovered in Thomas' stone-turning mind. His faith

---

6. True, Thomas was pessimistic about the future and his faith hadn't grasped the whole truth about Jesus, but what little he did grasp, he was willing to hang on to with his life.

twisted in silent convulsions touched off by the powerful uncertainties that mocked everything he believed. "Jesus a Messiah? He's dead! There is no kingdom. He was a fake and you've been a fool."

For three days all the disciples grieved, tormented by the doubts that possessed them. Then Jesus came.

> When therefore it was evening, on that day, the first day of the week, and when the doors were shut where the disciples were, for fear of the Jews, Jesus came and stood in their midst, and said to them, "Peace be with you." And when He had said this, He showed them both His hands and His side. The disciples therefore rejoiced when they saw the Lord. Jesus therefore said to them again, "Peace be with you; as the Father has sent Me, I also send you." . . .
> But Thomas, one of the twelve, called Didymus, was not with them when Jesus came. (vv. 19–21, 24)

Ever wonder why Thomas wasn't there? Probably because he had chosen to grieve alone. Reflective people usually do. They prefer solitude to crowded rooms for sorting out their questions.

Wherever that heartbroken disciple was, his companions soon found him and exclaimed, "We have seen the Lord!" (v. 25a). To which Thomas pessimistically replied,

> "Unless I shall see in His hands the imprint of the nails, and put my finger into the place of the nails, and put my hand into His side, I will not believe." (v. 25b)

Thomas could say nothing less. It would take more than words to help this reflective disciple overcome the disturbing lesson of having his master pinned to a cross with Roman spikes. It would take touching the resurrected Savior's wounds to heal the wounds in Thomas' faith. And that is exactly what Jesus allowed him to do.

> And after eight days again His disciples were inside, and Thomas with them. Jesus came, the doors having been shut, and stood in their midst, and said, "Peace be with you." Then He said to Thomas, "Reach here your finger, and see My hands; and reach here your hand, and put it into My side; and be not unbelieving, but believing." Thomas answered and said to Him, "My Lord and my God!" (vv. 26–28)

Now that—that is as raw an expression of sincere faith as you'll find anywhere. The kind of rock-solid faith that only comes to those who have honestly faced their doubts. And Thomas was such a person.

Afterward, Jesus extended a blessing upon those in the future whose doubts would be healed because they could touch His wounds with the hands of faith.

> Jesus said to him, "Because you have seen Me, have you believed? Blessed are they who did not see, and yet believed." (v. 29)

How Growth Occurs: "I Cannot Cope"

Throughout any life lived honestly and reflectively, there will be moments of doubt, times when we will feel that we cannot cope. How do we keep growing in the midst of those difficulties? By risking failure and not always playing it safe. By not placing our security in the temporal. By questioning and probing the uncertain, not blindly embracing the orthodox. And by admitting and struggling with our humanity, not denying our limitations and fears.

Nonreflective people ask, "What could be worse than unanswered questions?" Reflective people answer, "Unquestioned answers." Any question asked earnestly, without a hidden agenda, is not a skeptical question, it's an honest search. May we have the courage to never stop asking or searching!

 Living Insights STUDY ONE

Thomas possessed two great virtues found in all reflective people. First:

> He absolutely refused to say that he understood what he did not understand, or that he believed what he did not believe. There is an uncompromising honesty about him. He would never still his doubts by pretending that they did not exist. He was not the kind of man who would rattle off a creed without understanding what it was all about. Thomas had to be sure—and he was quite right.[7]

7. Barclay, *The Gospel of John*, p. 276.

How do you deal with your doubts? Do you attempt to still them by pretending they don't exist? Have you been raised to burn questions at the stake as heresy, or do you feel free to honestly admit when you don't understand something?

_____

_____

_____

_____

Thomas' second great virtue was that

> when he was sure, he went the whole way. "My Lord and my God!" said he. There was no halfway house about Thomas. He was not airing his doubts just for the sake of mental acrobatics; he doubted in order to become sure; and when he did, his surrender to certainty was complete. And when a man fights his way through his doubts to the conviction that Jesus Christ is Lord, he has attained to a certainty that the man who unthinkingly accepts things can never reach.[8]

Do you fight your way through doubts to firm convictions, or do you give up too soon?[9]

Admittedly, it's scary to consider abandoning those safe, secure creeds in order to face the doubts lurking in the shadows of our hearts. Confronting those niggling uncertainties feels almost like blasphemy . . . and what if the outcome isn't a sure conviction after all, but instead a muddled mess of questions?

Here are a couple of hands to hang on to as you fumble in the dark for answers. First, put your questions to resources you trust: the Bible, your pastor, reliable reference books. Second, keep in mind this reassuring verse of Scripture:

> And you will seek Me and find Me, when you search for Me with all your heart. (Jer. 29:13)

Remember, your journey is safe when your destination is Him.

8. Barclay, *The Gospel of John*, p. 277.

9. For further in-depth study, read *In Two Minds: The Dilemma of Doubt and How to Resolve It*, by Os Guinness, published by InterVarsity Press.

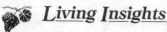 *Living Insights*

In times of deep pain and doubt, it's normal to withdraw, to want to be alone. But we must be careful not to isolate ourselves, for then we miss opportunities for God to minister to us through His Body. William Barclay writes,

> Because [Thomas] was not there with his fellow Christians he missed the first coming of Jesus. We miss a great deal when we separate ourselves from the Christian fellowship and try to be alone. . . . When sorrow comes and sadness envelops us, we often tend to shut ourselves up and refuse to meet people. That is the very time when, in spite of our sorrow, we should seek the fellowship of Christ's people, for it is there that we are likeliest of all to meet him face to face.[10]

When you struggle with doubts, do you naturally seek out other Christians for support, or do you tend to withdraw and become a shut-in?

_____

Is there perhaps a doubt that you're now struggling with which needs to be brought out of the closet and shared with some respected Christian friends, whom God could use to minister to you? This week, whom could you approach about this and when? Be specific.

_____

_____

_____

10. Barclay, *The Gospel of John*, p. 276.

Chapter 8

CHRIST AT THE CROSSROAD
OF ACCOMPLISHMENT

Luke 8:1–15

Red light. Wait, wait. Green. Accelerate, pass a few cars—red light. Wait, wait. Green. Go, stop, turn, stop, wait, pass, merge. That's city driving.

Wide-open, rolling hills of lush, green farmland; a grey ribbon of treelined, two-lane highway; wide-angle views of cloud-laced blue skies; open windows and fresh air. That's country driving.

Wouldn't it be great if all our driving could be done in the country? And wouldn't it be great if our journey through life could be on those relaxed rural roads with no stoplights and no crossings? Unfortunately, through most of our lives intersections follow one after the other, and we must stop, wait, and decide. Should I go straight? Right? Left? Make a U-turn?

These crisis points are significant because they force us to make decisions, they put us in motion, and they reveal the true nature of our character. One crossroad in particular affects us in those ways—and we may not even be aware of it. It is an unexpected intersection at the top of a mountain where we must open our hearts and examine our real motives. It is here that we reach the crossroad of accomplishment.

A Brief Analysis of Everyday Accomplishments

Accomplish simply means "to bring to completion: fulfill."[1] Whether it's a wartime politician signing a declaration of peace or an artist signing the bottom of a masterpiece, the result of accomplishment can be sweet or sour depending on how it's handled.

The Positive Side

Solomon gave us a taste of the positive side of accomplishment when he said, "Desire realized is sweet to the soul" (Prov. 13:19a).

---

1. *Webster's Ninth New Collegiate Dictionary,* see "accomplish."

The sense of satisfaction after even a small accomplishment is a wonderful feeling. A clean garage, a credit card account finally paid off, or a graduation after years of study are sweet experiences to be savored.

Accomplishment can also be a great inspiration to others. How many times have we read a biography of some remarkable man or woman, only to have their faith, courage, integrity, or sensitivity set us afire? Their character and the achievements born out of it spark in us a desire to live more fully and go beyond our fears to reach our dreams.

The Negative Side

On the darker side, however, accomplishments can lead to addiction. Desire's sweet realization can sour when enough is never enough. Proverbs 30:15–16 vividly illustrates the bitterness of insatiable craving.

> The leech has two daughters,
> "Give," "Give."
> There are three things that will not be satisfied,
> Four that will not say, "Enough":
> Sheol, and the barren womb,
> Earth that is never satisfied with water,
> And fire that never says, "Enough."

Rather than firing us with inspiration, the addiction to accomplishment consumes us with flames of frustration and drivenness. Henry Ward Beecher incisively observed, "Success is full of promise till men get it; and then it is a last-year's nest from which the birds have flown."[2]

Unfortunately, even the church struggles with this addiction. A preoccupation with numbers, buildings, growth, and size; an obsession with comparison; the unchecked drive to attract more and more—all are unmistakable signs of success's hold on today's ministries. But Christ never meant His church to be a slave to this merciless master. He meant us to walk in freedom, to attend to quality and not quantity. And He showed us this in the path He chose at the crossroad of accomplishment.

---

2. Henry Ward Beecher, as quoted in *The Home Book of Quotations*, 10th ed., comp. Burton Stevenson (New York, N.Y.: Dodd, Mead and Co., 1967), p. 1928.

A Biblical Synopsis of Jesus' Ministry

Never once in all Jesus' ministry do we see Him seized with panic. Though He faced a herculean task when He came to earth, His preparations were purposeful, and His ministry began quietly.

How It All Began

Foregoing strategy meetings and fund-raising campaigns, Jesus started out by first learning a trade and working at it for a decade or more. After leaving home, He entered the ministry quietly, being baptized by His cousin. He then carefully and deliberately chose twelve men in which to invest the rest of His life. Common men. Not cultured, robed, or degreed men, but ordinary fishermen and tax collectors (Mark 3:14)—just the opposite from today's "Star Search" mentality of ministry. Robert Coleman illuminates the vital difference in Christ's way of choosing disciples.

> What is more revealing about these men is that at first they do not impress us as being key men. None of them occupied prominent places in the Synagogue, nor did any of them belong to the Levitical priesthood. For the most part they were common laboring men, probably having no professional training beyond the rudiments of knowledge necessary for their vocation. . . . By any standard of sophisticated culture then and now they would surely be considered as a rather ragged aggregation of souls. . . . Not the kind of group one would expect to win the world for Christ.[3]

But for the next three years, this "ragged aggregation of souls" watched Jesus heal the sick, raise the dead, walk on water, and serve a banquet for five-thousand-plus out of a sack lunch. Without notebooks, seminars, or class notes, they learned how to do ministry. And the crowds grew.

Why Growth Occurred

Luke 8 reveals several reasons for the remarkable growth of Christ's ministry. First, He spoke and modeled the truth (v. 1). He

---

3. Robert E. Coleman, *The Master Plan of Evangelism*, 2d ed. (Old Tappan, N.J.: Fleming H. Revell Co., 1964), pp. 22–23.

had no hidden agendas; He simply "proclaim[ed] the kingdom of God." Second, He evidenced the power of God for all to see (v. 2). He entered the ranks of the disease- and demon-infested world and brought healing and deliverance, going where no scribe or Pharisee had gone before and giving the people a distinctively different message. And third, He had His needs met by the faithful support of loyal followers, as verse 3 states:

> And many others . . . were contributing to their sup-
> port out of their private means.

It's wonderful, isn't it? Nothing was forced or contrived; everything happened out of the natural flow of living. Jesus was not operating by some man-made growth strategy, yet growth occurred to such an extent that He no longer had to travel to the towns—the towns traveled to Him! Notice the contrast between verses 1 and 4:

> And it came about soon afterwards, that *He be-*
> *gan going about from one city and village to another*
> . . . (v. 1, emphasis added)

> And when a great multitude were coming together,
> and *those from the various cities were journeying to*
> *Him* . . . (v. 4, emphasis added)

Jesus' ministry had reached a peak. If He carefully planned His next moves, He would be at the top of the mountain. The entire world could be at His feet! This was an extremely critical and vulnerable moment.

When the Emphasis Changed

Instead of becoming hooked on more . . . bigger . . . larger . . . , Jesus faced the dangers that accompany an increase in numbers, and He did so by telling a parable He knew only a few would understand.

> "The sower went out to sow his seed; and as he
> sowed, some fell beside the road; and it was trampled
> under foot, and the birds of the air ate it up. And
> other seed fell on rocky soil, and as soon as it grew
> up, it withered away, because it had no moisture.
> And other seed fell among the thorns; and the thorns
> grew up with it, and choked it out. And other seed
> fell into the good soil, and grew up, and produced

a crop a hundred times as great." As He said these
things, He would call out, "He who has ears to hear,
let him hear." (vv. 5–8)

Why did He tell *this* parable? How did He expect to increase
His following when He told stories hardly anyone could grasp? Well,
the truth is that He wasn't trying to increase His following and
build a mega-ministry. He told this parable so that all those who
were just hangers-on might search their souls and get serious. He
decided it was time to thin the ranks, to purge and plant. Let's take
a brief look at the hidden meaning of what He was saying.

The parable has three essential ingredients: the sower, who
disburses the seed; the seed, which is the Word of God; and the
soil, which is the hearts and minds of His listeners. Jesus emphasizes
the condition of the soil because that is what determines the success
of the planting.

The soil by the road represents the hardened, unreceptive heart.
Over and over again, the seed hits the closed doors of this person's
mind and bounces away, leaving Satan to retrieve it so that the
person may not receive it and be saved (v. 12). The rocky soil is
the intellectually tolerant mind, those who are willing to hear the
Word but are unwilling to absorb and apply it (v. 13). The thorny
soil is like the busy churchgoer, who lets the important get choked
out by the nonessential (v. 14). And the good soil represents the
person with an open, willing heart, a faithful, persevering heart—
the heart Christ is looking for (v. 15).

What Ultimately Resulted

What in the world is the Lord doing telling a story like this? If
He ever had a chance to multiply the multitudes, now was the time!
He could have become the most popular preacher in the whole
Roman Empire, built buildings that would have put the Roman
temples to shame! He could have done all of this and more, *had
He been addicted to accomplishment.*

But He wasn't.

He never lost sight of His ultimate goal—to cultivate quality
of soil, not quantity.

A Few Analogies for Today

By this time you may be thinking that all growth in numbers is
bad. Please be assured, it is not. There is absolutely nothing wrong

with expansion or size—they are neutral things that only take their meaning from the motive behind them. The goodness or badness all depends on whether growth is the result of God's working or man's. Often, enlargement is a mark of God's blessing. But the trouble begins—the addiction emerges—when we develop a preoccupation with achievement and an ever-pressing need for our ministry to become larger. When that happens, we have taken a wrong turn at the crossroad of accomplishment.

How can we keep from becoming addicted to accomplishment? By keeping in mind three basics that will steady the euphoria of success.

First: *We need to pay attention to our primary assignment, which is to know Christ and walk with Him.* The essential issue when we face God someday will not be whether we drew the biggest crowd, but whether we daily walked with Jesus in obedience and faith. For by walking with Him, He can accomplish a great work *in* us.

Second: *We need to fulfill our primary activities as people of God.* From Luke's text we can infer at least three responsibilities of the Christian: (1) financially—to contribute to the support of a ministry we believe in out of our private means, (2) physically—to sow the seed and make Christ known, and (3) spiritually—to prepare and nurture the soil of our hearts. As we give our time and energy to each of these areas, God can accomplish great things *through* us.

Third: *We need to cultivate an attitude that pleases God.* At least four underlying attitudes are necessary in pleasing God: being sensitive to His Word when we hear it; being patient as we wait for Him—not ourselves—to produce fruit; being content while we wait until He acts; and being faithful to the end. When these attitudes flourish in our hearts, then God can accomplish His work *beyond* us and our efforts.

A Concluding Thought

If you are madly rushing to achieve more in life or in ministry, stop for a moment at your crossroad of accomplishment. Dig out the road map and rediscover God's goal for you. Learn to be content and patient traveling His roads; they may be lonely at times, or bumpy, or slower than others, but they are always going in the right direction.

And they're off!

Front doors spring open like starting gates, and millions of Americans bolt into the opening stretch, hoping to hit the first turn on the rail in prime position. Trying to get to the finish line with the most toys, perks, or pensions, their purpose is the same—to get ahead.

For some, the pressure to win constantly whips them so that they strain almost to the breaking point. A student at the University of Berkeley cracked under the pressure one day. "He ran through the library, shouting hysterically at his astonished fellow students, 'Stop! Stop! You're getting ahead of me!'"[4]

Has this kind of pressure been whipping you, making you strain almost to your breaking point? Have your accomplishments lost their sweetness and turned into bitter taskmasters instead? If they have, let's loosen the reins today so that you can once again—or perhaps for the first time—relax and enjoy the desires you *have* realized (Prov. 13:19a).

Let's begin by first exploring the dark side of accomplishment. Is there a particular accomplishment you have been racing for lately?

_____

_____

What does achieving this mean to you? Are you looking to it to give you value as a person? To give you the feeling of having "arrived"? To help you gain someone's long-withheld recognition and approval—maybe even love? What is your motive? Take your time to dig deeply here.

_____

_____

_____

_____

_____

4. Pamela Pettler, *Joy of Stress,* as quoted by Doug Sherman in *Keeping Your Head Up When Your Job's Got You Down* (Brentwood, Tenn.: Wolgemuth and Hyatt, Publishers, 1991), p. 43.

When you accomplish something like this, do you feel any lasting satisfaction?

_____

_____

If you aren't feeling any sweetness about your past accomplishments, what is it that makes you think driving for more will help?

_____

_____

_____

_____

Part of what makes accomplishment a dark, driven thing is that we try to make it do something it is not designed to do. If we try to make it the basis of self-worth, if we use it as a tool to impress others rather than as a joy to be shared, then we bind ourselves with cords of frustration and aching neediness because what it was designed to fill remains empty, and what it is trying to fill it cannot fit.

In overcoming the addiction to accomplishment, it will be crucial for you to learn the difference between what your accomplishments can and cannot do. Then you will be able to let achievement be what it should be from God's perspective; and you will also be able to fill those hungry needs of yours with the proper nourishment.

 ## Living Insights

One antidote to the addiction of accomplishment is contentment —a trait that comes anything but naturally to us. Even the great apostle Paul had to cultivate it: "*I have learned* to be content in whatever circumstances I am" (Phil. 4:11, emphasis added).

If Paul had to learn how to be content, there probably aren't any shortcuts for us. How can we cultivate this quality and break our accomplishment addiction? Let's start by examining four approaches to life that can free us from the shackles of our drivenness.

- **Living in the present.** Do you rush ahead to the future, driven by what-ifs? Are you uncomfortable being right where you are?

How can you stop sacrificing your present contentment on the altar of what might happen? What can you do to help yourself concentrate on being present in the moment?

_____

_____

_____

Seeking a calmer pace. Do you find yourself in a breathless rush most of the time? Do you finish one project and then hurry to the next, not even stopping to enjoy what you've done? What are some ways you can rein in your drivenness and seek calmness instead?

_____

_____

_____

Pursuing a lighter spirit. Does most of what you do feel like a life-or-death issue? Has life become so serious that a burdened intensity is your normal response to it? Are you afraid to fail, to be vulnerable? How would learning to laugh at yourself help?

_____

_____

_____

Cultivating a grateful heart. Do you take much of what others do for you for granted? Do you look on your own achievements as merely doing your duty? Have you thought about thanking God for giving you the talents, patience, and determination to achieve what you have? How do you think having a grateful attitude could help break the addiction to achieve?

_____

_____

_____

Chapter 9

CHRIST AT THE CROSSROAD OF DIVORCE

Matthew 19:3–12

Dearly beloved, we are assembled here in the sight of God and these witnesses to join together this man and this woman in the bonds of Holy Matrimony; which is an honorable estate, instituted of God. . . .

_____, wilt thou have this woman to be thy wedded wife, to live together after God's ordinance in the holy estate of matrimony? Wilt thou love her, comfort her, honor and keep her in plenty and in want, in joy and in sorrow, in sickness and in health, and, forsaking all others, keep thee only unto her, so long as ye both shall live?[1]

Deep down, in the privacy of your own heart, how would you answer that question if it were put to you today? Are you going through a particularly rough time in your marriage now? Many of us are. And to be honest, many of us aren't sure anymore if we would make that marriage vow. More than that, we are secretly entertaining the thought of divorce. Oh, at first we may have just toyed with the idea, but now we're in earnest—we want out.

In your heart, are you standing at the crossroad of divorce? Jesus is there too. He's aware of your pain and disappointment. He knows all the reasons you feel you should walk out. But before you do, would you be willing to let Him give you some frank advice?

For those of you willing to listen and who couldn't honestly answer "I will" to the marriage vow, we commend your courage and strength. And we pray that this lesson will add God's wisdom to your courage and strength to guide you in your crossroads decision.

---

1. *Minister's Manual* (Bradley, Ill.: Evangelical Church Alliance, 1982), pp. 54–55.

An Unguarded Declaration of the Issue

To fully understand Jesus' teaching on divorce, we must first go back to the biblical blueprints for marriage in Genesis 1–2.

How Did Marriage Begin?

"In the beginning God created the heavens and the earth" (Gen. 1:1); then light, seas, vegetation, stars, living creatures, and finally His crowning work, something that bore His unique signature.

> And God created man in His own image, in the image of God He created him; male and female He created them. (v. 27)

From the epic drama of chapter 1, Genesis 2 takes us behind the scenes for a closer look at Adam and Eve's creation and union.

> Then the Lord God formed man of dust from the ground, and breathed into his nostrils the breath of life; and man became a living being. . . .
> Then the Lord God said, "It is not good for the man to be alone; I will make him a helper suitable for him." . . . So the Lord God caused a deep sleep to fall upon the man, and he slept; then He took one of his ribs, and closed up the flesh at that place. And the Lord God fashioned into a woman the rib which He had taken from the man, and brought her to the man. (vv. 7, 18, 21–22)

The curtains then close on this incredible scene with God's timeless, never-to-be-improved-upon statement about marriage.

> For this cause a man shall leave his father and his mother, and shall cleave to his wife; and they shall become one flesh. And the man and his wife were both naked and were not ashamed. (vv. 24–25)

From this account we can glean at least three basic facts about marriage: It is to be between one man and one woman; the two are to be brought together by God; and they are to live out their lives for His glory.

But there's more. These same verses also reveal that God intended each marriage to possess four essential ingredients. First, *severance:* "A man shall leave his father and his mother." Both the husband and wife must separate from, and break dependent ties with, their parents or guardians. Second, *permanence:* "And shall cleave to his wife." *Cleave* means to bond together as one in a loyal and unwavering commitment. Third, *unity:* "They shall become one flesh." There is to be a unity, not uniformity, between spouses that allows both to fulfill their own distinct roles for a harmonious relationship. Fourth, *intimacy:* "The man and his wife were both naked and were not ashamed." The husband and wife are to enjoy the pleasures of emotional and physical intimacy.

That's how God designed the institution of marriage, as revealed in Genesis 1 and 2. But then the Fall of Genesis 3 followed like a wrecking ball which devastated that holy estate. And the foundational principle that seems to have been damaged worst is permanence.

What Has Happened to Its Permanence?

Sin has cut such a swath of destruction through marriage that today the happily married couple is an oddity. Vows like, "To have and to hold from this day forth, for better, for worse, for richer, for poorer, in sickness and in health, to love and to cherish, till death do us part"[2] have practically become meaningless, a joke. And the punch line is that half of all marriages in America end in divorce, with 65 percent of all remarriages ending the same way.[3]

Those figures include a great number of Christians, because divorce is now also fairly common in the church. More and more believers are seeking relief rather than a solution; they're choosing to walk away from their marriages instead of working through them. All of which leaves a catastrophic number of children who are casualties of divorce. Every year, one million children under the age of eighteen feel the destructive effects of divorce in the United States.[4] And many who do have two-parent homes are not living with both of their natural parents.

Why Be Concerned about It?

Obviously, there are many reasons we should be concerned about divorce and its ramifications. Ultimately, however, our greatest rea-

---

2. *Minister's Manual,* p. 56.

3. John Powell, S.J., *Happiness Is an Inside Job* (Valencia, Calif.: Tabor Publishing, 1989), p. 3.

4. Archibald D. Hart, *Healing Adult Children of Divorce* (Ann Arbor, Mich.: Servant Publications, Vine Books, 1991), p. 17.

son is simply that God is not pleased with divorce. Why? Because His plan clearly calls for there to be one woman with one man; for two parents of the opposite sex to rear their children; and for families to function with open communication, love, discipline, and security. And He wants His church to model these distinctives—not blur them with divorce.

Another crucial concern is that divorce starts a cycle that only gets worse. Once getting out becomes an option, the permanence of marriage is completely undermined. And history has shown that once a nation's homes are fractured, it's only a matter of time before that nation will teeter and collapse.

All this underscores the devastating effects of sin. Since the time of Genesis 3, all people have had to live out their marriages under sin's wrecking influence. Strife, abuse, wrath, low self-esteem, hatred, selfishness, immorality—mix all these into a marriage and it's easy to see why it takes the power of God to survive. It's easy to see why we should be concerned.

In Jesus' Day: His Instructions on Divorce

Jesus was certainly concerned about divorce, for even in His day it was rampant both among the common people as well as in the religious circles of the Pharisees. Let's join Christ now in Matthew 19, as the religious leaders put Him to the test on the crossroads question of divorce.

> And some Pharisees came to Him, testing Him, and
> saying, "Is it lawful for a man to divorce his wife for
> any cause at all?" (v. 3)

To fully comprehend the test behind the Pharisees' question, we must first understand an unusual law in Hebrew history and how it was interpreted in Jesus' day. Initially, God intended that Israel be His witness to the rest of the world. But the Jews of those bygone days instead floundered in unbelief. Because of their disobedience and intermarriage with other pagan races, Moses was permitted to release a certificate of divorce if "some indecency" was found in the marriage partner (see Deut. 24:1–4). This was to be the exception, however, and not the rule. As John R. W. Stott explains, divorce was "only a divine concession to human weakness."[5] It was never His original desire or plan.

5. John R. W. Stott, *The Message of the Sermon on the Mount (Matthew 5–7)*, rev. ed. of *Christian Counter-Culture*, The Bible Speaks Today series (Downers Grove, Ill.: InterVarsity Press, 1978), p. 95.

Various Answers

Now let's look at the differing interpretations of the phrase "some indecency," interpretations that sharply divided the people in Jesus' day. Commentator D. A. Carson writes:

> Opinion was divided roughly into two opposing camps: both the school of Hillel and the school of Shammai permitted divorce (of the woman by the man: the reverse was not considered) on the grounds of *'erwat dābār* ("something indecent," Deut. 24:1), but they disagreed on what "indecent" might include. Shammai and his followers interpreted the expression to refer to gross indecency, though not necessarily adultery; Hillel extended the meaning beyond sin to all kinds of real or imagined offenses, including an improperly cooked meal. Hillelite R. Akiba permitted divorce in case of a roving eye for prettier women.[6]

Put all this together and you can see why the Pharisees asked Jesus if a divorce could be obtained "for any cause at all." They were deliberately trying to draw Jesus into the Hillel-Shammai controversy, knowing that He would make enemies either way He answered and they might find grounds for condemning Him.

Rather than be pulled into that controversy, Jesus proceeded to align Himself with the prophet Malachi, who recorded God's own school of thought on divorce: "For I hate divorce" (Mal. 2:16). Despite all appearances, divorce is *not* normal, it is *not* neutral, nor is it the promised easy way out. It's destructive, and its consequences will injure generations.

Careful Analysis

Rather than argue the negative effects of divorce, however, Jesus began by reminding the Pharisees of God's positive design for marriage.

> And He answered and said, "Have you not read, that He who created them from the beginning made

---

6. D. A. Carson, "Matthew," in *The Expositor's Bible Commentary*, ed. Frank E. Gaebelein (Grand Rapids, Mich.: Zondervan Publishing House, Regency Reference Library, 1984), vol. 8, p. 411.

them male and female, and said, 'For this cause a man shall leave his father and mother, and shall cleave to his wife; and the two shall become one flesh'? Consequently they are no longer two, but one flesh." (Matt. 19:4–6a)

Then He drove home the permanence and sanctity of marriage with a powerful command.

"What therefore God has joined together, let no man separate." (v. 6b)

Still determined to embroil Jesus in the rabbinical debate, the Pharisees responded with, "Why then did Moses command to give her a certificate and divorce her?" (v. 7).

In answer to their question, Jesus makes three crucial distinctions, two of which are found in verse 8.

He said to them, "Because of your hardness of heart, Moses permitted you to divorce your wives; but from the beginning it has not been this way."

First, Jesus corrected the Pharisees: Moses didn't *command* divorce, he *permitted* it. Second, Jesus clarified the issue. Divorce was never in God's original plan —"but from the beginning it has not been this way." It's a secondary concession that was made because of the hardness of the human heart. Third, Jesus specified the meaning of "indecency," the controversial word in Deuteronomy 24:1 over which the liberal Hillels and strict Shammais had split.

"And I say to you, whoever divorces his wife, except for immorality, and marries another woman commits adultery." (v. 9)

In Greek, the term used here for *immorality* is *porneia*, from which we get our word *pornography*. *Porneia* has a lewd sexual connotation that is not limited to adultery, though it includes that. It can also refer to incest, homosexuality, or any type of sexual misconduct. That is, any type of sustained sexual misconduct.

It is doubtful that Jesus was giving permission to divorce over a one-night stand. That's not the meaning behind *porneia*. With this word, Jesus is referring to a continued unwillingness to remain sexually faithful to a marriage partner, an obvious determination to seek sexual contact outside of the marriage.

Even then, He is still not commanding the faithful partner to leave. Rather, every attempt should be made to first heal and hold that marriage together. Remember, reconciliation is the keynote of the gospel message—forgiveness and restoration between God and His beloved and between the beloved themselves. Should it be any less between husband and wife, those who proclaim the very mystery of Christ and His church (see Eph. 5:21–22)? However, if all serious efforts at reuniting fail, then, and only then, can a partner consider divorce.

Necessary Acceptance

We're not told whether the Pharisees grasped the seriousness of Jesus' teaching, but the disciples certainly did!

> The disciples said to Him, "If the relationship of the man with his wife is like this, it is better not to marry." (Matt. 19:10)

Keep in mind that the disciples had grown up with rabbis teaching ideas like, "A bad wife is like leprosy to her husband. What is the remedy? Let him divorce her and be cured of his leprosy."[7] In light of Jesus' emphasis on permanence, the disciples mistakenly felt that if divorce wasn't an option, then marriage should be avoided altogether. Jesus, however, patiently corrected them on the issue of abstinence from marriage.

> "Not all men can accept this statement, but only those to whom it has been given. For there are eunuchs who were born that way from their mother's womb; and there are eunuchs who were made eunuchs by men; and there are also eunuchs who made themselves eunuchs for the sake of the kingdom of heaven. He who is able to accept this, let him accept it." (vv. 11–12)

In other words, if you have the gift of celibacy, that's wonderful; accept it. But if you choose to marry, take it seriously—make it permanent.

---

7. William Barclay, *The Gospel of Matthew*, vol. 2, rev. ed., The Daily Study Bible Series (Philadelphia, Pa.: Westminster Press, 1975), p. 206.

Some Hard-to-Hear Conclusions That Call for a Response

As you ponder Christ's counsel at the crossroad of divorce, here are three important thoughts to remember. First: *The sanctity of marriage necessitates commitment.* Romantic love is wonderful, but only a solid commitment to marriage will enable it to last during those times when the romance wears thin. Second: *The necessity of commitment is weakened by depravity.* Selfishness, abuse, infidelity, arguments, sarcasm—all the sins we loose in our marriages constantly weaken the bond of commitment. Third: *The depravity of humanity is counteracted only by Christ.* Without Jesus, a solid marriage is virtually impossible. He alone can provide the grace and strength we need to overcome the destructive effects of sin and truly love one another in lasting relationships.

> _____, wilt thou have this man to be thy wedded husband, to live together after God's ordinance in the holy estate of matrimony? Wilt thou love him, honor him, cherish and comfort him in plenty and in want, in joy and in sorrow, in sickness and in health, and, forsaking all others, keep thee only unto him, so long as ye both shall live?[8]

What will you answer?

 Living Insights

How long has it been since you exchanged your wedding vows? Were they like these?

> I, _____, take thee, _____, to be my wedded wife/husband, to have and to hold from this day forth, for better, for worse, for richer, for poorer, in sickness and in health, to love and to cherish, till death do us part, according to God's holy ordinance; and thereto I plight thee my troth.[9]

If you're like most, those vows haven't been repeated since your wedding day. In fact, many of you probably can't even remember

8. *Minister's Manual,* p. 55.
9. *Minister's Manual,* p. 56.

what you said or heard. Now, since you were helplessly in love, and it was hot, and the soloist was singing the wrong song—it's understandable. But perhaps now, when the romance has evened out and you're more realistic about life and each other, perhaps now more than ever you need to reaffirm what you vowed before God and others.

A beautiful way of protecting the permanence of your marriage is to plan a special time to renew your wedding vows. Would you be willing to do that?

Maybe you could return to the place where you were married or got engaged. If not, could you stir up some creative juices and recreate the atmosphere some other way? Why not ask your best man and maid of honor to share in this with you? Use the space provided to brainstorm together on what you might do.

_____

_____

_____

_____

_____

If you truly can't remember the vows you exchanged at your wedding, feel free to use the traditional one at the beginning of this Living Insight. Or perhaps write a new one that would reflect the maturing of your love and life together, as well as the essential ingredients we learned about today: severance, permanence, unity, and intimacy.

 Living Insights

In our lesson, we concluded that without Christ a solid marriage is virtually impossible. Does this mean that because a husband and wife know Jesus they will automatically have a wonderful, committed marriage? No. But you would be surprised at how many of us naively think so. One of the gravest mistakes couples make is to assume that, because they are Christians, divorce could never happen to them. But the apostle Paul warns, "Therefore let him who thinks he stands take heed lest he fall" (1 Cor. 10:12).

For the next few moments, let's take heed of how we're following Christ in our marriages lest we fall into divorce.

When was the last time you prayed with your spouse? Are you praying together regularly?

_____

_____

Are you really aware of the areas in which your spouse is struggling to obey Christ right now? Does he or she know how you are doing? Be as specific as possible.

_____

_____

_____

_____

_____

What more could be done to make Christ the center of your marriage?

_____

_____

_____

_____

_____

_____

Some of you reading this Living Insight would love to be able to pray with your spouse, but first you need help just getting your husband or wife to come home again, to stop some form of abuse, or to leave an affair. If this describes you, please buy or borrow Dr. James Dobson's book *Love Must Be Tough*, published by Word. This book is specifically written to comfort and guide the partner who is struggling to hold a marriage together.[10]

10. For further study, read *Men and Women: Enjoying the Difference*, by Larry Crabb, Zondervan Publishing House.

Chapter 10

CHRIST AT THE CROSSROAD
OF REMARRIAGE
Matthew 19:9; 1 Corinthians 7:8–16, 39; 2 Corinthians 5:16–17

If divorce is one of the most painful crossroads to stand in, then remarriage is one of the most tentative.

Biblical scholars, wise counselors, and compassionate friends all give advice and opinions that often leave us with a muddle of questions instead of solid help. Some say remarriage is permissible in any situation—even blessed under God's grace—while others prohibit it altogether.

As we seek Christ's heart on this issue, let's proceed prayerfully, asking God for clear guidance in this very sensitive area.

Scriptural Survey of the Possibility of Remarriage

In turning to the Scriptures, we'll find three separate cases in which remarriage is permissible.[1] Our first is in Matthew 19, familiar territory we explored in our last lesson.

An Unrepentant, Immoral Partner

As you'll recall, when the Pharisees questioned Jesus concerning the grounds for divorce, He answered,

> "And I say to you, whoever divorces his wife, except for immorality, and marries another woman commits adultery." (v. 9)

Christ hates divorce. But He also hates to see the marriage bond desecrated by spouses who continually pursue promiscuous life-styles and are unwilling to repent. In situations such as these, Jesus allows the faithful partner the option to divorce and remarry.

Desertion by an Unbelieving Mate

The second case in which remarriage is permissible is found in 1 Corinthians 7. But before we examine this particular case, we need to understand the context surrounding it.

1. This chapter assumes the reader understands that death is another permissible reason for remarriage (see 1 Cor. 7:39).

In the first seven verses, the apostle Paul basically states that, if he had his choice, he would prefer that all people remain unmarried in order to dedicate their lives to the undistracted service of God. He realizes, though, that not everyone has the gift of celibacy, so those who don't should by all means marry.

In the rest of the chapter, Paul describes three categories of people and how each group should approach the issue of marriage and remarriage. This first group, found in verses 8–9, is made up of the unmarried and widows. His preference for them, also, is that they remain single like himself; but if they cannot, they, too, should marry.

The next category is the married, and to them Paul says to stay married, as we see in verses 10–11. But within these verses we find an important sidelight on another critical topic. Let's take a little time to look at this passage.

> But to the married I give instructions, not I, but the
> Lord, that the wife should not leave her husband
> (but if she does leave, let her remain unmarried, or
> else be reconciled to her husband), and that the
> husband should not send his wife away.

As we saw in our last lesson, Jesus' primary concern in dealing with divorce was the permanence of marriage. Paul reiterates that here, when he says that "the wife should not leave her husband." His parenthetical comment, however, addresses the reality of trouble and provides us with a course of remedy—separation. Sometimes a partner truly cannot stay and remain sane. Sometimes a person's life is at stake. Sometimes, for the sake of the children, it becomes necessary to flee. In these desperate situations, separation is permitted, not to file for divorce, but to seek help and attempt to reconcile the marriage.[2]

Now we come to the third category, and the particular case of remarriage we want to look into today. This group, which Paul calls "the rest" (v. 12), concerns those in unequally yoked marriages—where a believer is married to an unbeliever. Again, Paul would have those who are married stay that way, unequally yoked or not. And in this case especially, it is important to stay together because the believer can exert a godly, sanctifying influence in the home

2. For further reading on abusive behavior, we suggest the following books: Carolyn Koons' *Beyond Betrayal*, Harper and Row Publishers; and Grant Martin's *Please Don't Hurt Me*, Victor Books.

(vv. 12–14). However, sometimes an unbelieving mate will abandon the marriage, which is the topic of verse 15.

> Yet if the unbelieving one leaves, let him leave; the brother or the sister is not under bondage in such cases, but God has called us to peace.

There are three vital points for us to remember from this verse. First, it is the unbeliever who voluntarily abandons the marriage. Second, the believing partner is told, "let him leave." Attempting to *coerce* the unbeliever to either leave or stay is wrong. And third, the believer who has been deserted is "not under bondage."

In order to understand what "not under bondage" means, we must look ahead to verse 39. Here Paul writes that "a wife is *bound* as long as her husband lives" (emphasis added). But if her husband dies? The bond is broken and she is free to remarry. In the same way, Paul says, when a believer is abandoned by an unbeliever, that believer is "not under bondage"; the bond of that marriage has been broken, freeing the believer to pursue remarriage. Commentator R. C. H. Lenski adds further insight into the meaning of the broken bond.

> From that day onward the fetters of the marriage tie have been broken and remain so, now and indefinitely. The deserting spouse broke them. No law binds the believing spouse. . . . It goes without saying that a believing spouse will by Christian kindness and persuasion do all that can be done to prevent a rupture. But when these fail, Paul's verdict is: "Thou art free!"
>
> Desertion is exactly like adultery in its effect. Both disrupt the marriage tie. . . . The essence of marriage is union. When this is disrupted, the union which God intended to be a permanent one is destroyed, sinfully destroyed. There is only this difference in the case of adultery, the innocent spouse may forgive and continue the marriage, or may accept the dire result, the sundering of the marriage. In the case of desertion the former is not possible; the deserted spouse can no longer continue a marriage, for none exists.[3]

3. R. C. H. Lenski, *The Interpretation of St. Paul's First and Second Epistles to the Corinthians*, (1937; reprint, Minneapolis, Minn.: Augsburg Publishing House, 1961), p. 295.

Marital Failure Prior to Salvation

Our final case concerning remarriage is found in 2 Corinthians 5.

> Therefore from now on we recognize no man accord-
> ing to the flesh; even though we have known Christ
> according to the flesh, yet now we know Him thus
> no longer. Therefore if any man is in Christ, he is
> a new creature; the old things passed away; behold,
> new things have come. (vv. 16–17)

The Greek term for *new* that Paul uses twice in verse 17 is *kainos*, meaning a brand-new, fresh creation.[4] Paraphrased, the first half of this verse states, "If anyone is a Christian, he or she becomes a fresh creation." Christ has forgiven all our former sins and has removed them "as far as the east is from the west" (Ps. 103:12). And that includes our past marital failures. Regardless of how many times an unbeliever may have divorced, Paul says "the old is passed away." Jesus has made us *kainos*, a new creation free to begin life and marriage anew in obedience to Him.

Practical Warnings to All Who Are Married—or Hope to Be

In our search to understand when remarriage is permissible, we must be careful that we do not forget the one foundational issue underlying all our discussions—the seriousness of marriage itself. Author Mike Mason reminds us,

> While it may seem to be just one more cog in the
> machinery of social order, in point of fact there is
> nothing else in secular society which comes even
> close to the seriousness, the all-pervasiveness, the
> indissolubility and sheer daring of marriage.[5]

As a further reminder, here are four important exhortations to remember. First, to the unmarried: *Be patient!* Some of us will remain contentedly single all our lives, and that's great. Others ache for a marriage partner, and that's great too. Only don't let that desire hurry you; take time to carefully choose a mate.

---

4. Grammarian W. E. Vine defines *kainos* as "that which is unaccustomed or unused, not new in time, recent, but new as to form or quality, of different nature from what is contrasted as old." This same word can also be found in John 13:34, Ephesians 4:24, and Revelation 2:17.

5. Mike Mason, *The Mystery of Marriage* (Portland, Oreg.: Multnomah Press, 1985), p. 74.

Second, to the married: *Be content!* Stay in your marriage, culti-vate your relationship, and honor your vows. Trust in the sovereign God to provide you with the strength you need to patiently endure and build a strong marriage.

Third, to the miserable who have the right to end a marriage and remarry: *Be careful . . . be wise!* Recognize that you're extremely vulnerable because of the intense need you have for a loving rela-tionship. Go slowly, and get wise counsel lest you fall for the first person who comes along—someone whose only redeeming quality is that he or she is available.

Fourth, to the remarried: *Be grateful and understanding!* Enjoy the new bond that you've entered into and make it last. But be aware that there are some Christians who will not accept or affirm anyone who has been remarried regardless of how biblically permis-sible the union is. When you encounter such opposition, just keep entrusting yourself to Christ, and He will open doors in places where you can be ministered to and minister with His blessing!

 Living Insights

In these two Living Insights, we're going to test your knowledge and understanding of divorce and remarriage by having you play the role of "Dear Counselor." Imagining that the following letters were sent to you, write a reply to each explaining the biblical options concerning divorce and remarriage. Ready?

Dear Counselor,

I don't know what to do. Both my husband and I are Christians. Bob is also a deacon at church and well respected. He is a really good man, but he gets out of control sometimes when he's angry. I know he doesn't mean it, and he always apologizes later, but I'm afraid of what might happen one of these times. The abuse seems to be getting worse, espe-cially since he lost his job two months ago. Yester-day, for example, he exploded when I asked him about our finances and hit me several times. Then he threatened to leave me if I told anyone. What should I do?

_____

_____

_____

_____

Dear Counselor,

My whole world has been turned upside-down
since my best friend told me my wife was having an
affair. When I confronted her about this, she denied
it at first, and I believed her. Yesterday, though, I
was given irrefutable evidence that she had, in fact,
slept with a fellow from our church choir! I confronted her again, and she admitted to the deed.
She says it was only a one-time thing and that afterwards she felt guilty and stopped. But how can I
believe what she says? I have never felt so humiliated
and angry in my life. First she has an affair with
another "Christian," and then she lies to me about
it! What should I do?

_____

_____

_____

_____

 ## Living Insights

Let's continue our counseling to those struggling with marriage
issues.

Dear Counselor,

I've been a Christian now for about two years.
During this time I've tried hard to go to church and
read my Bible and pray. The more I do, however,
the worse things seem to get between my husband
and me. Half the time he acts like he can't stand
to be around me, and the other half, he seems to

enjoy making fun of my faith in front of our non-Christian friends. In all our ten years of marriage, things have never been so bad. Still, I love my husband and don't want a divorce. So when Bill threatened to leave me if I didn't quit "preaching" and going to church, I agreed to stop. What do you think?

_____

_____

_____

_____

Dear Counselor,

I am really confused about marriage, which will seem obvious when I tell you that I've been married and divorced twice. I'll admit I never really tried to make my first marriage work. I got pregnant, and my folks basically forced me to marry the guy. I felt trapped and angry and took it out on him in the worst ways. Three months later, when I had a miscarriage, I signed the divorce papers before I even left the hospital. After that I was determined to never marry again. But then I met Dave. He was so kind and thoughtful that, after living together for a short while, I agreed to marry him. Two children later, he left me for another woman who "could meet his needs better." It was during the awful time of that second divorce that I came to know Christ through a friend. Since then I have been active in a local church and growing spiritually. Can someone like me, who has had two husbands already, marry another with God's blessing? What do you think?

_____

_____

_____

_____

Chapter 11

CHRIST AT THE CROSSROAD OF CONFRONTATION

Matthew 16:21–23; Luke 22:31–34, 47–62

"Experience is the best teacher." At least that's what a certain husband said to himself as he spread out the materials to build his first brick wall. But a few hours and several aspirins later, thumbing through the yellow pages for a good brick mason, he mumbled to himself, "Experience is the best teacher all right—it taught me to stay out of the bricklaying business!"

What this frustrated homeowner discovered was that experience alone can only teach you so much. It is *guided* experience that is really the best teacher because it adds one key factor: confrontation.

Confrontation is the piano teacher nagging you to curve your fingers, the ski instructor picking you out of the snow and reminding you not to cross your tips. Without this healthy and constructive confrontation, learning would stop. And the world would be full of flat-fingered pianists and flat-nosed skiers!

Unfortunately, confrontation is often thought of as something negative—an ugly scene with fur flying and feelings foundering. This is probably because many of us have been on the receiving end of someone who knew how to *affront* better than *confront*. But Scripture, thankfully, shows us a different meaning of the word, a meaning that can help us build a solid understanding of the do's and don'ts of this essential process.

Gaining an Understanding of Confrontation

Although the word *confrontation* does not appear in Scripture, the concept is there in both the Old Testament and the New. The first of at least five synonyms is *reproof*.

> He is on the path of life who heeds instruction,
> But he who forsakes reproof goes astray.
> (Prov. 10:17; see also 12:1)

The second synonym is *rebuke*, which is a little sterner than *reproof* but contains the same element of confrontation.

A rebuke goes deeper into one who has
    understanding
Than a hundred blows into a fool. (17:10)

Next, also from Proverbs, is the word *wounds.*

Faithful are the wounds of a friend,[1]
But deceitful are the kisses of an enemy. (27:6)

Confrontation is a "wounding." Let's face it—it hurts. But when it comes from a friend, someone who has our best interests at heart, we can trust that it is necessary.

Another synonym is *correct,* which carries the idea of confronting to improve, to rescue from the wrong course and put safely on the right one.

Correct your son, and he will give you comfort;
He will also delight your soul. (29:17)

The last word we'll look at is *discipline,* which is found in the New Testament letter to the Hebrews.

But He disciplines us for our good, that we may
share His holiness. All discipline for the moment
seems not to be joyful, but sorrowful; yet to those
who have been trained by it, afterwards it yields the
peaceful fruit of righteousness. (12:10b–11; see also
vv. 5–10a)

What It Means

All of these words and their nuances of meaning give us a composite picture of what confrontation should be.

Confrontation is speaking the truth
in a personal, face-to-face encounter
with someone we love
regarding an issue
that needs attention or correction.

---

1. The original Hebrew uses a causative stem in the first phrase, which would actually render it: "Faithful are the bruises caused by the wounding of one who loves you." How important it is to see that not everyone has the right to "wound" another! Some in the body of Christ feel they have the "spiritual gift" of confrontation. But that is not true. The secret revealed in this verse is that only a friend has the right to wound us; we are much more open to someone who we *know* loves us, understands us, and cares for us.

This looks pretty simple on paper, but it really isn't. Confrontation, which always seeks to build up rather than tear down, is an art to be learned.

How It Works

Before we look at the four major components of confrontation, we need to remember one crucial thing: confrontation should be done privately, away from the curious and unsympathetic eye of the public. It may need to be painful, but it need never be embarrassing (compare Matt. 7:12).

With this in mind, let's look at the first component. When confronting someone, state the issue tactfully and directly. Like surgery, confrontation must be precise and clean. We don't want to prolong the pain or make the incision bigger than we have to through vague perceptions and thoughtless wording.

Second, provide examples—without exaggerating. Clear, accurate examples will help the person understand why change is needed.

Third, suggest a plan of action. Don't just dump a load of facts and illustrations on the person; rather, try to help your friend find a way to correct the problem.

Finally, and most importantly, reassure your friend of your concern, compassion, and care throughout the entire process. If you miss this, you will only be accusing and attacking, and the harm from that could be irreparable.

Principles like these are usually easier to digest when we can see them in action. So let's turn to the Master, who dealt with confrontation throughout His life, and learn from His example.

Observing It in Action: Christ and Peter

As Jesus drew nearer and nearer to the Crucifixion, His crossroad of confrontation intensified. Three passages show conflicts involving one of His own disciples, Peter, a man Jesus loved and who deeply loved his Master in return. In each of these episodes, we will see Jesus chiseling and shaping Peter, taking him from a roughedged and raw disciple to a perfectly cut stone for the foundation of the church. Through His sculpting process, we will learn when, why, and how to confront.

When to Confront—Matthew 16:21–23

The first scene opens soberly, in the shadow of the Cross.

> From that time Jesus Christ began to show His
> disciples that He must go to Jerusalem, and suffer
> many things from the elders and chief priests and
> scribes, and be killed, and be raised up on the third
> day. (v. 21)

Up until now, the disciples had assumed that Jesus would establish a literal kingdom on earth. The idea of a suffering Messiah was
foreign to them, even shocking. So Peter, never one to keep quiet,
"flung a protecting arm round Jesus, as if to hold him back from a
suicidal course."[2]

> And Peter took Him aside and began to rebuke Him,
> saying, "God forbid it, Lord! This shall never hap-
> pen to You." (v. 22)

To be sure, Peter thought he had Jesus' best interests at heart.
But he didn't. And Jesus immediately confronted him with the
devastating implication of his words:

> "Get behind Me, Satan! You are a stumbling block
> to Me; for you are not setting your mind on God's
> interests, but man's." (v. 23)

Just moments earlier, Peter had been affirmed as a "rock" (v. 18),
but now he was a "stumbling block," a Satan-like tempter and
snare. For in his rebuke to Christ, he was actually urging Him to
put His own interests above God's—to forsake the way of the Cross.
And this, Christ could not allow.

From Jesus' confrontation with Peter, we can glean two answers
to our question of when to confront. First, when people become
stumbling blocks to us or others. And second, when people have
set their minds on man's interests, not God's.

Why to Confront—Luke 22:31–34

The next episode with Peter takes place the evening before the
Crucifixion. In the quiet of the Upper Room, Jesus had given His
last lesson on servanthood, concluding it with a glorious picture of
the future (Luke 22:24–30). But His next words took an abrupt
shift as He turned to address Peter.

---

2. William Barclay, *The Gospel of Matthew,* vol. 2, rev. ed., The Daily Study Bible Series
(Philadelphia, Pa.: Westminster Press, 1975), p. 148.

"Simon, Simon, behold, Satan has demanded
permission to sift you like wheat; but I have prayed for
you, that your faith may not fail; and you, when once
you have turned again, strengthen your brothers."[3]
(vv. 31–32)

In effect, Jesus was telling Peter that he was in the cross hairs
of Satan's scope; he was the adversary's special target. And though
Jesus reassured him that He had prayed for him, He also gave Peter
the disturbing prediction that he would stumble, though not fall
away completely. Peter's response?

"Lord, with You I am ready to go both to prison and
to death!" (v. 33)

Me? Fail? Impossible! Peter's overconfidence left him wide open
for Satan's attack; and seeing the danger, Christ quickly confronted
his imperiled disciple.

"I say to you, Peter, the cock will not crow today
until you have denied three times that you know
Me." (v. 34)

Christ's humbling warning reveals two reasons we should confront. First, to strengthen areas of vulnerability. And second, to
soften overconfidence and warn of blind spots. We want to protect
those we love, even from themselves.

The next episodes between Jesus and Peter take place the night
before the Crucifixion. In the predawn darkness, Jesus would have
to confront His disciple—along with the religious leaders—again.
In these scenes, we will see how He went about it.

How to Confront—Luke 22:47–62

After the somber Passover meal, and after an agonizing time of
prayer in the Garden of Gethsemane, Jesus and His men looked up
to see a string of flickering torchlights wending their way toward
them. At the head of the crowd is Judas, the murderous traitor who
would turn their Lord over to a mob. This was more than the
disciples could stand.

---

3. Jesus used the plural form of "you" first, meaning that Satan wanted to severely test all
the disciples, not just Peter. Then Jesus switched to the singular "you," telling Peter that
He was praying specifically for him.

And when those who were around Him saw what
was going to happen, they said, "Lord, shall we strike
with the sword?" (v. 49)

Not waiting for an answer, a certain disciple wielded his sword
and aimed for the closest enemy, cutting off the ear of the high
priest's slave (v. 50). Who was that impetuous one? Who else but
Peter (John 18:10). But Jesus immediately took control, confronting
His zealous disciple.

"Stop! No more of this." And He touched [the slave's]
ear and healed him. (Luke 22:51)

After stilling Peter's violence, Jesus turned His attention to the
bloodthirstiness of the religious leaders.

And Jesus said to the chief priests and officers of the
temple and elders who had come against Him, "Have
you come out with swords and clubs as against a
robber? While I was with you daily in the temple,
you did not lay hands on Me; but this hour and the
power of darkness are yours." (vv. 52–53)

The power of darkness was theirs, and they arrested Jesus, bringing Him to the house of the high priest. Following at a distance
was Peter; not overconfident now, but nervous, frightened. And in
that fear he did what would have once been unthinkable—he denied his Lord (vv. 54–60). At that moment, as the cock crowed,

the Lord turned and looked at Peter. And Peter remembered the word of the Lord, how He had told
him, "Before a cock crows today, you will deny Me
three times." And he went out and wept bitterly.
(vv. 61–62)

Step back a moment from the intensity of these scenes, and
look at Jesus' actions. They reveal four methods of confrontation:
(1) an abrupt, passionate command—"Stop! No more of this" (v. 51);
(2) a thought-provoking question—"Have you come out with swords
and clubs as against a robber?" (v. 52); (3) a well-worded, analytical
statement—"While I was with you daily in the temple, you did not
lay hands on Me; but this hour and the power of darkness are yours"
(v. 53); and (4) a mere look—"The Lord turned and looked at Peter"
(v. 61). Sometimes a look speaks more than any words could do.

94

The Next Time You Need to Confront

As you continue to learn the art of confrontation, keep in mind three essentials.

Be sure. Be sure you really have a good reason. Confrontations should be rare—don't think of them as a daily discipline. Make sure that this process is what's really needed.

Be specific. Be specific about your purpose; dig around in your soul until you know exactly why you feel you should confront someone.

Be sensitive. Be sensitive with the way you do it; make sure the method fits the person's needs—not your agenda. Watch your timing and choose your words, or looks, carefully.

Confronting a friend may be the hardest thing we've ever done, but if we love someone, we'll care too much to keep quiet.

 Living Insights

The title of the book *Caring Enough to Confront* captures the essence of confrontation. In fact, the author even refers to confronting as "care-fronting," because caring for the needs of others should be the basis of any confrontation. Unfortunately, however, when we face a situation in which confrontation is needed, we often think about our own needs first. And that tendency undermines the effectiveness of confrontation.

Self-centered types of confrontation usually take one of four approaches:

- First, the aggressive "I'll get him" approach.

- Second, the scared "I'll get out" approach.

- Third, the doormat "I'll give in" method.

- And fourth, the compromising "I'll meet you halfway" method.[4]

None of these approaches are productive . . . and worse, they often result in great damage. Be honest now, do you tend to gravitate toward one of these approaches? If so, which one?

---

4. David Augsburger, *Caring Enough to Confront*, rev. ed. (Ventura, Calif.: GL Publications, Regal Books, 1981), pp. 13–15.

Let's get a little more specific. Think of a particular conflict from your recent past that you don't feel you handled so well. What type of approach did you use? How did you feel afterward, and how did the other person respond?

_____

_____

_____

How could you have handled the situation differently? Think back to what we learned about the when, the why, and the how of confrontation.

_____

_____

_____

For more detailed help on honing your confrontation skills, read David Augsburger's fine book *Caring Enough to Confront.*

 ## Living Insights

STUDY TWO

Kimberly knew she must do something. Her dad had left a note on the refrigerator a few weeks before, saying good-bye; and although she understood that he wanted to divorce her mom, there had to be one last chance to change his heart. So she decided to write him a letter.

In the letter, she pictured the family riding in a brand-new car: Mom and Dad in the front, she and her brother in the back. But then the car, like the family, started riding roughly—shaking and rattling. Next, strangely, Dad was not driving anymore. Mom was at the wheel, and Dad was gone. Then she wrote:

> It was nighttime, and we had just turned the corner near our house. Suddenly, we all looked up and saw another car, out of control, heading straight for us. Mom tried to swerve out of the way, but the other car still smashed into us. The impact sent us flying off the road and crashing into a lamppost.

The thing is, Dad, just before being hit, we could see that you were driving the other car. And we saw something else: Sitting next to you was another woman.[5]

The letter went on to describe the family's injuries and to ask the heart-wrenching questions: "Are you all right? Are you hurting from the wreck? Do you need us like we need you? If you need me, I'm here and I love you."[6]

As a result of that letter of confrontation, her dad was so moved that he came home and, through counseling, restored the marriage. What was so effective about that daughter's letter? She used an *emotional word picture* that illustrated her pain, the impact of her father's sin, and her unconditional love for him.

Emotional word pictures can communicate powerfully in a confrontation situation. If you feel that you need to confront someone, try framing your words in a picture like Kimberly did. Use the following space to write out your ideas.

_____

_____

_____

_____

_____

_____

_____

_____

Techniques for developing emotional word pictures are found in a book by Gary Smalley and John Trent called *The Language of Love.* We recommend this book to help you voice your feelings when you have to confront someone, or when you simply want to say that you care.

5. Gary Smalley and John Trent, *The Language of Love* (Pomona, Calif.: Focus on the Family Publishing, 1988), p. 14.

6. Smalley and Trent, *The Language of Love,* p. 15.

Chapter 12

CHRIST AT THE CROSSROAD OF PAIN

Matthew 26:36–44, 57, 67; 27:2, 28–30, 33–35, 45–46

Lord of Hosts. Bright Morning Star. Chief Shepherd. These are but a few of the many wonderful names for Jesus. He's also known as the

Wonderful Counselor
Anointed of God
Alpha and Omega
Mighty God
Almighty
Prince
King
Lion
Man of Sorrows

Wait . . . Man of Sorrows? That's supposed to be wonderful? Well, to those of us at a crossroad of pain, it is probably the most welcome and comforting name of all.

Coming to an Understanding of Pain

Perhaps this picture of Christ is new to you. Maybe you can't imagine Him as being weak or sad, or struggling with hurts like yours. If so, the prophet Isaiah is just the person to help you get acquainted with the One above all others who understands your pain . . . the Man of Sorrows.

As It Relates to Jesus' Life

Seven centuries before Jesus' birth, Isaiah wrote one of the most powerful chapters in the Old Testament concerning the Messiah. In it he introduced Him to us as the "man of sorrows," using practically every synonym available for suffering. Let's pick up the graphic description in Isaiah 53:3–4.

> He was despised and forsaken of men,
> A man of sorrows, and acquainted with grief;

And like one from whom men hide their face,
He was despised, and we did not esteem Him.
Surely our griefs He Himself bore,
And our sorrows He carried;
Yet we ourselves esteemed Him stricken,
Smitten of God, and afflicted.

In Hebrew, the root word used in both verses for "sorrows" is *kaab*, which means "to be in pain." Literally, Jesus was a "Man of pains." And as you read on through verse 12, Isaiah catalogues still more of His sufferings.

- Pierced, crushed, chastened, scourged (v. 5)

- Oppressed, afflicted, led to slaughter (v. 7)

- Put to grief (v. 10)

- Anguished (v. 11)

- Poured out to death (v. 12)

That is what Isaiah predicted about Jesus before His birth, and this is what the author of Hebrews remembered about Him after His death:

> In the days of His flesh, He offered up both prayers
> and supplications with loud crying and tears to the
> One able to save Him from death, and He was heard
> because of His piety. (Heb. 5:7)

Everything we've seen thus far, from the swollen list of hurts in Isaiah to the weeping in Hebrews, has to do with one word—*pain*. Webster defines it as "a basic bodily sensation induced by a noxious stimulus, received by naked nerve endings, characterized by physical discomfort . . . acute mental or emotional distress."[1] In the truest sense of the word, Jesus was a man of naked, nerve-jarring physical, mental, emotional, and spiritual pain.

As It Relates to Our Lives

From the moment we're born to the moment we die, pain seldom leaves us, and we never quit trying to leave it. But pain does have some redeeming qualities. Physically, for example, it warns us

---

1. *Webster's Ninth New Collegiate Dictionary,* see "pain."

when something is wrong and tells us precisely where. On a spiritual level, we learn obedience from the things we suffer, just as Jesus did (Heb. 5:8), and the pain of trials strengthens us to become mature people of faith (see James 1:2–4).

Noting the benefits of pain, however, doesn't subtract one throbbing moment of it from our lives. And we're not suggesting it should. Neither are we attempting to belittle your pain by comparing it to Christ's. Rather, our purpose is to let you know that if you're feeling despised, forsaken, crushed, or afflicted, Jesus can sympathize (Heb. 4:15). How much can He sympathize? Let's look at the Gospel passages that flesh out the stark bones of Isaiah's prophecies.

Focusing on the Ordeal at Gethsemane and Golgotha

At the beginning of Jesus' public ministry, John the Baptizer pointed to Him and said, "Behold, the Lamb of God who takes away the sin of the world!" (John 1:29). Those are wonderful words for you and me, but stop and think how Jesus must have felt when He heard them. They probably sent a pang of nerve-wrenching dread through His heart as they reminded Him of the hour when He would be led to the slaughter on our behalf. As we go back to that hour, to that cup of suffering from which Christ would drink deeply, let's consider the types of pain this Man of Sorrows endured.

Relational Pain

According to Matthew 26:30, Jesus and His disciples ended their last supper together with a hymn. Were there tears in His eyes and a tightness in His throat as He sang the last stanza with Peter, James, John, and the others He loved so dearly? The Twelve had little notion of the pain and confusion about to overtake them. But Jesus knew. And He also knew, as they headed toward Gethsemane and His darkest hour, that if ever He needed their supportive presence, it was now.

> Then Jesus came with them to a place called Gethsemane, and said to His disciples, "Sit here while I go over there and pray." And He took with Him Peter and the two sons of Zebedee, and began to be grieved and distressed. Then He said to them, "My soul is deeply grieved, to the point of death; remain here and keep watch with Me." (vv. 36–38)

100

The pain was too much to bear alone, even for Jesus, so He sought comfort and support in His most intimate friends. Only then did He attempt to pray through His raging struggle.

> And He went a little beyond them, and fell on His face and prayed, saying, "My Father, if it is possible, let this cup pass from Me; yet not as I will, but as Thou wilt." (v. 39)

How deep was the pain? Deep enough for Jesus to plead for a way out, a way around this hour. Deep enough for Luke, in his gospel account, to describe Christ's agony as a fight for His very life, with His sweat dripping so profusely that it looked like blood trickling from a wound (Luke 22:44).

Drenched by the pain that seized His soul, Jesus came away from the battle momentarily to be encouraged by His friends. But just when He needed them the most, they failed Him.

> And He came to the disciples and found them sleeping, and said to Peter, "So, you men could not keep watch with Me for one hour? Keep watching and praying, that you may not enter into temptation; the spirit is willing, but the flesh is weak." He went away again a second time and prayed, saying, "My Father, if this cannot pass away unless I drink it, Thy will be done." And again He came and found them sleeping, for their eyes were heavy. And He left them again, and went away and prayed a third time, saying the same thing once more. Then He came to the disciples, and said to them, "Are you still sleeping and taking your rest?" (Matt. 26:40–45a)

Three times Jesus returned for some needed encouragement and companionship, only to find that His best friends had none to give. Not one stayed awake to comfort or to pray for Him. He was all alone with only His pain for company.

Internal Pain

Jesus had known His whole life that this one awful hour would come, but knowing didn't change His feelings. When it finally arrived, His internal agony was so great that He fell on His face and earnestly prayed—not once, not twice, but three times—for God to let that cup pass (vv. 39, 42, 44). Jesus pleaded for another way; He wanted to know if something, anything, could be done to avoid this crossroad of pain. His grief in the Garden was raw, terrible; the thought of experiencing God's wrath for our sins sickened Him. The terror and suffering of that hour ravaged His soul to the point of death. It was internal pain beyond any our human souls have ever known.

Physical Pain

But there's more, much more. When Judas arrived, flanked by a great multitude armed with swords and clubs, the disciples fled. And that marked the beginning of the physical brutalities. We see the list in Matthew 26–27.

- He was seized and no doubt roughly treated like a common criminal. (26:57)

- Some spat in His face, others slapped and beat Him. (26:67)

- He was bound again, and then later scourged according to the other gospel writers. (27:2; see Mark 15:15; John 19:1)

- They pressed thorns in the shape of a crown onto His head and mocked Him. (27:29)

- Again, they spat on Him and then beat Him with a reed. (27:30)

- They crucified Him, driving spikes into His hands and feet. (27:33–35a)

Ultimate Pain

As horrible as Jesus' relational, internal, and physical pain was, the worst of His suffering was still to come. Matthew writes:

> Now from the sixth hour darkness fell upon all the land until the ninth hour. And about the ninth hour Jesus cried out with a loud voice, saying, "Eli, Eli, lama sabachthani?" that is, "My God, My God, why hast Thou forsaken Me?" (27:45–46)

The ultimate hour of pain for Jesus was when He fulfilled John the Baptizer's words and became the Lamb of God who bore all our sins. At that time God turned His back on His only Son, leaving Him to face the full wrath for our sins, while nailed to a cross, naked and alone. That's total abandonment, and it was His ultimate pain.

Drawing Analogies between Christ's Pain and Ours

Man of Sorrows. Perhaps now you can see why that name is the most welcome and comforting one to someone at a crossroad of pain. It's a name that identifies with our suffering, and it is also a name that holds out the promise of understanding, companionship, and relief. So the next time you feel pain's noxious, nerve-rending presence, remember the following truths.

Relationally, no one stays closer than Christ. No one is more caring or more readily available. He is better than the most faithful husband, more understanding than the most compassionate wife. And when all others have fled or forgotten you, He will still be there to keep watch with you through your darkest night.

Internally, no one can heal us on a deeper level than Christ. Knowledge alone cannot always mend the deep emotional pains we feel. Shame, guilt, disappointment, grief—the Man of Sorrows is acquainted with them all. And He can strengthen us as we experience them in our lives.

Physically, no one comforts better than Christ. His hand on your life in a time of affliction may not send the disease away, but it is amazing how His hand can soothe.

Ultimately, no one sees the benefits of our pain more clearly than Christ. He can see the rewards that await us if we will only continue to trust in Him. Rewards such as wisdom, maturity, hope, faith, peace . . . and ultimately a crown of eternal life.

> "And He shall wipe away every tear from their eyes;
> and there shall no longer be any death; there shall
> no longer be any mourning, or crying, or pain; the
> first things have passed away." (Rev. 21:4)

 Living Insights

Relationally, do you feel forgotten and alone? Internally, are you struggling with shame, grief, disappointment, or fear? Physically, is there a specific handicap, sickness, or injury that causes you intense pain? Ultimately, are you wondering if God has left you? Using the four categories from our lesson, take a few minutes to identify the kinds of pain that you're struggling with now.

Relational _____

_____

Internal _____

_____

Physical _____

_____

Ultimate _____

_____

Let's continue exploring these areas in our next study.

 Living Insights

In *Where Is God When It Hurts?*, author Philip Yancey writes:

> It seems to me that suffering involves two main issues: 1) whoever *caused* my discomfort, and 2) my *response*. Most of us expend our energy trying to figure out the cause of our pain before we'll decide how to respond. Joni Eareckson . . . consumed two years exploring possible causes of her accident. But, as Joni found, to the extent that we concentrate on cause, we may well end up embittered against God.
>
> In Job, the portion of the Bible which most vividly poses the question "Who causes pain?" God deliberately sidesteps the issue. He never explained the cause to Job. All the way through, the Bible steers from the issue of cause to the issue of response. Pain and suffering have happened—*now* what will you do? The great discussers of cause, Job's three friends, are dismissed with a scowl. The Bible is so clear on this point that I must conclude the real issue before Christians is not "Is God responsible?" but "How should I react now that this terrible thing has happened?"[2]

2. Philip Yancey, *Where Is God When It Hurts?* (Grand Rapids, Mich.: Zondervan Publishing House, 1977), p. 85.

How have you reacted to the terrible things that have happened to you? Are you still trying to determine whether God is responsible before you'll decide how to respond? Think through these questions in light of the pain you explored in Study One.

Relational _____

_____

Internal _____

_____

Physical _____

_____

Ultimate _____

_____

Is there an area of pain and suffering where your focus has been more on finding a cosmic cause than on choosing a healthy response? This week commit yourself to changing your focus and allowing the Man of Sorrows to bring His healing touch to your pain.

Chapter 13

CHRIST AT THE CROSSROAD OF PREJUDICE

Selected Scriptures

In the early 1960s, people were shocked by the controversial book *Black Like Me*. It was written by John Howard Griffin—a white man who became black. After shaving his hair and temporarily changing his skin color through a series of medical treatments, the author then walked, hitchhiked, and rode buses through a number of states in the Deep South. His goal was to gather scientific data on blacks in that part of the country; but in the end, he filed that information away and published instead the journal he kept of his experiences.

In this journal he traced "the changes that occur to heart and body and intelligence when a so-called first-class citizen is cast on the junkheap of second-class citizenship."[1] He had found that many people who normally would have treated him with courtesy and gracious hospitality subjected him instead to insults, mistreatment, and a hate so raw it could only be described as violent. For Griffin had walked, hitchhiked, and ridden buses straight into a crossroad of prejudice. Listen to the preface of his book.

> The Negro. The South. These are details. The real story is the universal one of men who destroy the souls and bodies of other men (and in the process destroy themselves) for reasons neither really understands. It is the story of the persecuted, the defrauded, the feared and detested. I could have been a Jew in Germany, a Mexican in a number of states, or a member of any "inferior" group. Only the details would have differed. The story would be the same.[2]

To be completely fair about this volatile subject, we should also note that prejudice is always found on both sides. Yes, there are

---

1. John Howard Griffin, *Black Like Me*, 2d ed. (Boston, Mass.: Houghton Mifflin Co., 1977), preface.

2. Griffin, *Black Like Me*, preface.

whites against blacks, but there are also blacks against whites. There are rich against poor and poor against rich. Men against women and women against men. Gentiles against Jews and Jews against Gentiles. Protestants against Catholics and Catholics against Protestants. On and on we could go, for it exists between every continent, culture, and class of people.

And very few of us seem inclined to give up our prejudices. Rather, we stubbornly defend them with all kinds of irrational rationales, from unfounded Bible doctrines to unproven scientific theories. As philosopher William James once wrote, the basic human tendency is to obstinately

> keep unaltered as much of our old knowledge, as
> many of our old prejudices and beliefs, as we can.
> We patch and tinker more than we renew.[3]

As you explore this crossroad in our lesson today, pray that it will challenge you to do more than "patch and tinker" with any prejudices you might have. With Christ's help, may it lead you to be "renewed in the spirit of your mind, and [able to] put on the new self, which in the likeness of God has been created in righteousness and holiness of the truth" (Eph. 4:23–24).

Prejudice Defined and Observed

In Mark 7, Jesus revealed prejudice to be a heart problem.

> "For from within, out of the heart of men, proceed
> the evil thoughts, fornications, thefts, murders, adul-
> teries, deeds of coveting and wickedness, as well as
> deceit, sensuality, envy, slander, pride and foolish-
> ness. All these evil things proceed from within and
> defile the man." (vv. 21–23)

You may not find the word *prejudice* specifically listed here or anywhere else in the Bible, but you will see the categories under which it falls—"evil thoughts," "deeds of wickedness," "deceit," "slander," "pride," and "foolishness."[4] It is conceived in the realm

---

3. William James, as quoted in *Bartlett's Familiar Quotations*, 15th ed., rev. and enl., ed. Emily Morison Beck (Boston, Mass.: Little, Brown and Co., 1980), p. 650.

4. Scripture does use the words *partial* and *partiality*. For further study, read Leviticus 19:15; Deuteronomy 1:17; 10:17; Proverbs 28:21; Matthew 22:16; Romans 2:11; James 2:9.

of the thought life, is given birth in mean-spirited slander, then comes to frightful maturity in acts of hatred and cruelty.

Technical Definition

Webster defines prejudice as "injury or damage resulting from some judgment or action of another in disregard of one's rights; *esp:* detriment to one's legal rights or claims . . . an irrational attitude of hostility directed against an individual, a group, a race, or their supposed characteristics."[5] In its root form, it simply means to prejudge, to form an opinion prematurely on the basis of preconceived ideas.

General Observations

Let's move from the theological and technical side of prejudice now and note three of its general characteristics. First, it is a learned trait—none of us is born with prejudice. Yes, we are born with sin natures, but the specific biases we hold are ones that are passed on to us, usually from someone older.

Second, it keeps us in darkness. In Matthew 6, Jesus said:

> "The lamp of the body is the eye; if therefore your eye is clear, your whole body will be full of light. But if your eye is bad, your whole body will be full of darkness. If therefore the light that is in you is darkness, how great is the darkness!" (vv. 22–23)

Our eyes—meaning our ability to perceive and discern truth—are like windows through which light enters our hearts and souls. When those windows are begrimed with prejudice, the light is obscured and darkness fills the heart. The mind then blindly bases its judgments on a reality that is only dimly perceived or not seen at all.

Third, it binds us to the old, closing out the possibility of the new and innovative. As William Barclay illustrates:

> Almost all new discoveries have had to fight their way against unreasonable prejudice. When Sir James Simpson discovered the virtues of chloroform he had to fight against the prejudice of the medical and religious world of his day. One of his biographers writes: "Prejudice, the crippling determination to walk only in time-worn paths, and to eschew new

---

5. *Webster's Ninth New Collegiate Dictionary,* see "prejudice."

ways, rose up against it, and did their best to smother the new-found blessing."[6]

Never was this more true than in Jesus' day. For when the Messiah came, prejudice reared its ugly head and did its best to smother the newfound blessing by nailing Him to a cross.

Its Presence in Jesus' Day

Before we look at the prejudice that led to Christ's crucifixion, let's briefly note some of the biases that dominated the people and events of His day.

Geographical Prejudice

In the first century, Palestine was only 120 miles long. To the extreme north lay Galilee, to the extreme south, Judea, and in the middle was Samaria. Because of a centuries-old feud, the Samaritans and the Jews deeply hated one another. The racial tension was so high, in fact, that when Jews traveled from either Galilee to Judea or Judea to Galilee, they went completely around Samaria. The detour doubled their travel time, but to a people who considered being called a Samaritan a gross insult (see John 8:48), it was worth it.

Jesus didn't join either side in this racial feud, however; when He left Judea for Galilee, He simply passed right through the forbidden territory (4:3–4). Along the way, He stopped at a well in the Samaritan village of Sychar and asked a woman for a drink. Hear the incredulity and astonishment in her voice as she grapples with the racial implications of His request.

> "How is it that You, being a Jew, ask me for a drink since I am a Samaritan woman?" (For Jews have no dealings with Samaritans.) (v. 9)

As is plain to see by the woman's response, Palestine was locked in an intense geographical prejudice. Stronger still, however, was the political prejudice that existed between the Jews and the Romans.

Political Prejudice

In Matthew 22, the Pharisees tried to embroil Jesus in one of the hot political issues of the day with the question, "Is it lawful to give a poll-tax to Caesar, or not?" (v. 17b).

6. William Barclay, *The Gospel of Matthew,* vol. 1, rev. ed., The Daily Study Bible Series (Philadelphia, Pa.: Westminster Press, 1975), pp. 243–44.

The controversy surrounding this question is rooted in the fact that Palestine was under Roman rule at the time—and the Jews hated it! Not only because their freedom was taken away, but also because they were required to pay taxes to Caesar.

According to Roman law, every Jew was required to pay a ground tax, an income tax, and a poll tax. The amount due for this third tax was one denarius, a little over a day's wage, and was paid with a tribute coin bearing Caesar's image.

For the Jew, however, Jehovah was the only true king, and to pay any kind of tribute to a godless, non-Jewish Caesar was to affirm his rule and insult God. That's what made the poll tax issue so volatile—it reflected Rome's political prejudice against Israel.

Religious Prejudice

A third major area of prejudice in Palestine was religion. Not only was there friction between the monotheistic Jews and the poly-theistic Romans, but there was also friction between Jesus' teachings and the teachings of Israel's religious leaders. As you will see in our following lesson on hypocrisy, Jesus scathingly condemned the scribes and Pharisees as hypocrites, blind guides, fools, and whitewashed tombs (Matt. 23). And that was all from just one conversation! Many other heated exchanges took place that left the scribes and Pharisees seething with hatred.

Prejudice at the Trials and Crucifixion of the Savior

It was that hatred, that deep-seated prejudice against Jesus, that ultimately instigated His crucifixion.

Where It Emerged

> Then the chief priests and the elders of the people were gathered together in the court of the high priest, named Caiaphas; and they plotted together to seize Jesus by stealth, and kill Him. (Matt. 26:3–4)

Israel's most "holy" men plotted the death of Jehovah's sinless Son. Though it may seem incredible at first, it really isn't when you understand the power of prejudice. Remember, prejudice shuts out the light. And in its darkness people have committed the most heinous of crimes—including what you're about to read.

What It Caused

With their souls in total darkness now, the chief priests sought any possible way to incriminate Jesus so that they could legally put

Him to death. But they had a hard time finding any mud to sling, until two men came forward, panting and yelling, "Listen to this! You won't believe what this guy told us. He said he could destroy the temple of God and rebuild it in three days!" (vv. 59–61).

This was the chance the priests had been waiting for. It was finally time for a face-off.

> And the high priest stood up and said to Jesus, "Do You make no answer? What is it that these men are testifying against You?" But Jesus kept silent. And the high priest said to Him, "I adjure You by the living God, that You tell us whether You are the Christ, the Son of God." Jesus said to him, "You have said it yourself; nevertheless I tell you, hereafter you shall see the Son of Man sitting at the right hand of Power, and coming on the clouds of heaven." Then the high priest tore his robes, saying, "He has blasphemed! What further need do we have of witnesses? Behold, you have now heard the blasphemy; what do you think?" They answered and said, "He is deserving of death!" Then they spat in His face and beat Him with their fists; and others slapped Him, and said, "Prophesy to us, You Christ; who is the one who hit You?" (vv. 63–68)

Because the Jews were not allowed by Roman law to put anyone to death, they were forced to take Jesus before Pilate (27:1–2). In doing so, they had to change the trumped-up charge from blasphemy to treason, a crime punishable by death according to Roman standards. And to make this charge plausible, they accused Jesus of claiming to be a king, a potential usurper to Caesar's throne.

Pilate questioned Jesus about that charge and many others, but in the end he found nothing deserving of death (vv. 11–23). His efforts to release Jesus, however, were thwarted by the riotous lunacy of a prejudiced mob who willingly accepted the responsibility of Jesus' death (vv. 25–26).

How Jesus Dealt with It

Throughout this terrible ordeal, Jesus refused to dignify the prejudiced lies and accusations with a reply. Instead, He kept silent, not answering a single charge (26:63; 27:12, 14).

111

Conclusion

Years later, looking back on that awful hour, the apostle Peter wrote:

> For what credit is there if, when you sin and are harshly treated, you endure it with patience? But if when you do what is right and suffer for it you patiently endure it, this finds favor with God. For you have been called for this purpose, since Christ also suffered for you, leaving you an example for you to follow in His steps, who committed no sin, nor was any deceit found in His mouth; and while being reviled, He did not revile in return; while suffering, He uttered no threats, but kept entrusting Himself to Him who judges righteously. (1 Pet. 2:20–23)

Have you, like Jesus and John Howard Griffin, been "persecuted, defrauded, feared, and detested"? Then keep entrusting yourself to "Him who judges righteously," because that Judge has experienced the humiliation, the cruelty, and the pain of this crossroad and will comfort those who trust in Him (2 Cor. 1:3–4). For God Himself reassures us of His power and worthiness to hold our trust:

> "Listen to Me, you who know righteousness,
> A people in whose heart is My law;
> Do not fear the reproach of man,
> Neither be dismayed at their revilings.
> For the moth will eat them like a garment,
> And the grub will eat them like wool.
> But My righteousness shall be forever,
> And My salvation to all generations. . . .
> I, even I, am He who comforts you.
> Who are you that you are afraid of man who dies,
> And of the son of man who is made like grass;
> That you have forgotten the Lord your Maker,
> Who stretched out the heavens,
> And laid the foundations of the earth;
> That you fear continually all day long because of
>   the fury of the oppressor,
> As he makes ready to destroy?
> But where is the fury of the oppressor? . . .
> For I am the Lord your God, who stirs up the sea

and its waves roar (the Lord of hosts is His name).
And I have put My words in your mouth, and have
covered you with the shadow of My hand, to estab-
lish the heavens, to found the earth, and to say to
Zion, 'You are My people.'"
(Isa. 51:7–8, 12–13, 15–16)

 ## Living Insights

Prejudice is powerful. It's tragic, it's cruel, and it knows no
bounds. The religious leaders of Jesus' day proved that. So did the
educated Nazis who tended their gardens while butchering eleven
million men, women, and children. So did Stalin, whose political
juggernaut put thirty million to death.

Such overwhelming, faceless numbers make it easy to become
numb to the real horror of prejudice. And it's easy, too, to think
that we would never do such evil, letting ourselves off the hook.
But we all have prejudices. And though ours may not create the
same monstrous numerical consequences of a Hitler or a Stalin,
they do share the same basic, depraved traits that Jesus revealed in
Mark 7:21–22.

Does your obedience to the royal law of loving your neighbor
as yourself transcend race, geography, and class? Or are you only
willing to follow Christ right up to the border of Samaria, but not
into it? Take some time now to identify any prejudices you might
be wrestling with.

_____

_____

_____

_____

If your eyes are stained with prejudice, consider the powerful
truth of the following words from C. S. Lewis, then write down
how seeing others as he proposes might help cleanse you of your
prejudice.

> There are no *ordinary* people. You have never talked
> to a mere mortal. Nations, cultures, arts, civilization
> —these are mortal, and their life is to ours as the life

of a gnat. But it is immortals whom we joke with, work with, marry, snub, and exploit—immortal horrors or everlasting splendours. . . . Next to the Blessed Sacrament itself, your neighbor is the holiest object presented to your senses. If he is your Christian neighbour he is holy in almost the same way, for in him also Christ . . . the glorifier and the glorified, Glory Himself, is truly hidden.[7]

_____

_____

_____

_____

 ## Living Insights

In his book *A Legacy of Hatred,* David A. Rausch writes:

> Are Christians really different from the rest of society? Some Christians throughout Europe not only opposed the Nazis but also helped and defended the Jewish people. They met the challenge that was suddenly thrust upon them. However, they were relatively few in number—a fact that perplexed Richard Gutteridge as he studied German evangelical response to Nazi racist propaganda. Gutteridge concluded: "Most tragically of all, what was missing was a spontaneous outburst at any point by ordinary decent Christian folk, who certainly existed in considerable numbers."[8]

We "ordinary decent Christian folk" still exist in considerable numbers today. But are we standing up and protesting against the prejudices of our day? Or are we passively embracing them as those Christians in Germany did in the late thirties and early forties?

7. C. S. Lewis, *The Weight of Glory,* rev. and enl., ed. Walter Hooper (New York, N.Y.: Macmillan Publishing Co., 1980), p. 19.

8. David A. Rausch, *A Legacy of Hatred: Why Christians Must Not Forget the Holocaust,* 2d ed. (Grand Rapids, Mich.: Baker Book House, 1990), p. 5.

When someone tells a racist joke, do you politely but firmly reject such slander? Or do you simply nod a shy smile and say nothing?

Does prejudice make your blood boil, or are you not really bothered by it unless it affects you directly?

Prejudice is rampant today. And as Rausch points out, it seems to be growing.

> Organized racism presents a challenge facing each American today. As our country has gone through a period of economic instability, a resurgence of prejudice and hatred is erupting in an alarming number of racial incidents and forming insidious hate groups. Daily it becomes less possible to ignore blatant racism as it knocks at the doors of our cities, our schools, and our churches.[9]

Brothers and sisters in Christ, this is a wake-up call to a very serious problem. One that we must actively oppose in whatever way we can. And in our efforts to oppose the problem, let's not forget to lend a helping hand to its victims. For as Christ said,

> " 'Truly I say to you, to the extent that you did it to one of these brothers of Mine, even the least of them, you did it to Me.' " (Matt. 25:40; see also vv. 31–46)

9. Rausch, A Legacy of Hatred, p. 8.

Chapter 14

CHRIST AT THE CROSSROAD OF HYPOCRISY

Matthew 6:1–5, 16; 15:1–2, 6–9

How many times have you heard non-Christians joke about Christianity because of the flagrant hypocrisy they see? How many disillusioned believers have you known whose faith has floundered because of being cheated or lied to by religious hypocrites? And what about the fellow in the wheelchair with cerebral palsy who was asked to leave a church because the members were afraid he might have a "fit"? Hypocrisy.

To many people, being a Christian and being a hypocrite are one and the same. One individual summed it up this way:

> A Christian is a man who feels repentance on a Sunday for what he did on Saturday and is going to do on Monday.[1]

Perhaps the greatest tragedy of all is the disparaging connection of hypocrisy with today's ministers. An epidemic of phoniness and deceit has ravaged the trust and respect people have had in church leaders.

Religious artificiality among religious leaders is nothing new, however. It was rampant even in Jesus' day, and He unleashed His strongest words on those who were responsible. Seven times in Matthew 23 Christ witheringly denounced Israel's teachers with, "Woe to you, scribes and Pharisees, hypocrites" (vv. 13, 14, 15, 23, 25, 27, 29). But that wasn't all. He also blasted them as "blind guides" (v. 16), "fools" (v. 17), "whitewashed tombs" (v. 27). And in verse 33 He delivered this stinging condemnation:

> "You serpents, you brood of vipers, how shall you escape the sentence of hell?"

Jesus was livid about the hypocrisy of those high-profile imposters because "they say things, and do not do them" (v. 3), and

---

1. Thomas R. Ybarra, as quoted by Laurence J. Peter in *Peter's Quotations* (New York, N.Y.: William Morrow and Co., Bantam Books, 1977), p. 84.

because even when they did do something, "they do all their deeds to be noticed by men" (v. 5).

Explanation: Hypocrisy Exposed

In Greek, the word Jesus used to portray the scribes and Pharisees is *hupokritēs*. Originally, it meant "one who answers back," such as an orator or someone who recited poetry. Later, as Greek theater developed, this same term became synonymous for actors who assumed different roles in a play by wearing different oversized masks. Eventually, however, the term took on the negative connotation that Jesus used to refer to anyone in real life who hid behind a mask or played a part.

Such pretending to be what one is not is consistently condemned in the Scriptures. In Isaiah, for example, the Lord decries the people's hollow lip service, distant hearts, and rote reverence (29:13–14). Over in Romans, Paul wrote, "Let love be without hypocrisy" (12:9). He commands us to not be phony, to live what we say we believe. Even the apostle Peter had to be painfully reminded of this once. For while he preached that all believers, Jew and Gentile alike, were one in Christ, his conduct in the city of Antioch completely denied this truth. He played the role of a *hupokritēs*, which brought Paul center stage with a stern confrontation (see Gal. 2:11–14).[2]

The most powerful words about this subject, however, come from the outraged lips of our Lord. Far from the image of "gentle Jesus, meek and mild," Jesus is here brutally honest and unyielding with the sin of hypocrisy. Let's turn now to Matthew 6, the crossroads passage of our study.

Amplification: Hypocrisy Illustrated

It was during His Sermon on the Mount, a call to the life of simple, authentic faith, that Jesus paused to issue this stern warning:

> "Beware of practicing your righteousness before men to be noticed by them; otherwise you have no reward with your Father who is in heaven." (v. 1)

To a first-century Jew, the three fundamental ways of "practicing righteousness" were almsgiving, praying, and fasting. And, as we

---

2. See also James 1:21–22; 3:13–17; and 1 Peter 2:1–3.

117

shall see, Jesus never disputes the importance of these; rather, He cautions against practicing them as the hypocrites do and then gives instructions on the right way to model each one.

First, the problem of pious almsgiving to impress others.

Giving

> "When therefore you give alms, do not sound a trumpet before you, as the hypocrites do in the synagogues and in the streets, that they may be honored by men. Truly I say to you, they have their reward in full." (v. 2)

Hypocrites love to give publicly so that they can be honored publicly. Their primary interest isn't in meeting a need but in putting their own generosity on display. And this kind of giving to impress others not only displeases God, it also forfeits any future reward we might have received from Him. How, then, should we give?

> "But when you give alms, do not let your left hand know what your right hand is doing that your alms may be in secret; and your Father who sees in secret will repay you." (vv. 3–4)

Humble, righteous giving is characterized by *spontaneity*, not always giving the same amount on the same day; by *anonymity*, not announcing or parading your gift for others to see; and by *hilarity*, not with an attitude of grim duty, but with overflowing joy! God promises to remember and reward our giving when it is marked by these three traits (see also Heb. 6:10).

In a similar way, Jesus warns against hypocrisy in one of our most significant spiritual disciplines: prayer.

Praying

> "And when you pray, you are not to be as the hypocrites; for they love to stand and pray in the synagogues and on the street corners, in order to be seen by men. Truly I say to you, they have their reward in full." (Matt. 6:5)

In Jesus' day, prayer had degenerated in five areas. First, it had become a formal exercise rather than a free expression of the heart. There were standardized, routine prayers for every occasion. Second, prayer was ritualistic. Everyone prayed in prescribed places at prescribed times: 9:00 A.M., 12:00 P.M., and 3:00 P.M. Third, prayers were long and wordy. The more eloquent and flowery the words, the better a prayer was judged to be. One well-known prayer, for example, had no less than sixteen adjectives preceding the name of God. Fourth, prayer was often reduced to meaningless repetition of the same word or phrase. And fifth, praying had become a cause for pride rather than humble communication in a sacred relationship.

According to one source, "praying well" had become a legalistic status symbol, performed with an ostentatious public display of outstretched hands, bowed heads, and eloquent words uttered loudly three times a day—preferably on a busy street corner.[3] How, then, are we to pray?

> "But you, when you pray, go into your inner room, and when you have shut your door, pray to your Father who is in secret, and your Father who sees in secret will repay you. And when you are praying, do not use meaningless repetition, as the Gentiles do, for they suppose that they will be heard for their many words. Therefore do not be like them; for your Father knows what you need, before you ask Him." (vv. 6–8)

True prayer is not to be playacted before an audience but sincerely poured out before the Lord in private. It is to be personal, real, natural—not feigned with long, empty phrases. And, according to verses 14–15 of this same chapter, we're not to harbor grudges when we pray.[4]

Beginning in Matthew 6:16, Jesus then goes on to deal with the hypocrisy commonly displayed in the third expression of piety: fasting.

Fasting

> "And whenever you fast, do not put on a gloomy face as the hypocrites do, for they neglect their appearance in order to be seen fasting by men. Truly I say to you, they have their reward in full." (v. 16)

---

3. William Barclay, *The Gospel of Matthew*, vol. 1, rev. ed., The Daily Study Bible Series (Philadelphia, Pa.: Westminster Press, 1975), p. 197.

4. In Psalm 66:18, the psalmist goes so far as to say, "If I regard wickedness in my heart, The Lord will not hear [my prayer]."

Just how bad was the hypocrisy surrounding fasting? Commentator William Barclay wrote:

> The Jewish days of fasting were Monday and Thursday. These were market days, and . . . the result was that those who were ostentatiously fasting would on those days have a bigger audience to see and admire their piety. There were many who took deliberate steps to see that others could not miss the fact that they were fasting. They walked through the streets with hair deliberately unkempt and dishevelled, with clothes deliberately soiled and disarrayed. They even went the length of deliberately whitening their faces to accentuate their paleness.[5]

Though we typically associate pride with showy displays of prosperity, there can also be pride in sanctimonious displays of extreme humility and asceticism. How, then, are we to fast?

> "But you, when you fast, anoint your head, and wash your face so that you may not be seen fasting by men, but by your Father who is in secret; and your Father who sees in secret will repay you." (vv. 17–18)

Finally, let's turn to Matthew 15 and note yet another side of the scribes and Pharisees' hypocrisy.

Embracing Tradition

> Then some Pharisees and scribes came to Jesus from Jerusalem, saying, "Why do Your disciples transgress the tradition of the elders? For they do not wash their hands when they eat bread." (vv. 1–2)

Notice that the scribes and Pharisees didn't say the disciples had transgressed the Law of Moses. It was the "tradition of the elders" they were concerned about, a large body of oral teachings on the Mosaic Law that they had created over generations and that they regarded as having the same authority, if not more, than the Scriptures.

In this particular instance, they were concerned about the disciples' failure to obey the elders' tradition in regard to the washing

---

5. Barclay, *The Gospel of Matthew*, p. 235.

of hands before a meal. To help you appreciate just how extreme the scribes and Pharisees had become in their rules, here's just one of the many elaborate washings they expected everyone to observe.

> Water jars were kept ready to be used before a meal. The minimum amount of water to be used was a quarter of a log, which is defined as enough to fill one and a half egg-shells. The water was first poured on both hands, held with the fingers pointed upwards, and must run up the arm as far as the wrist. It must drop off from the wrist, for the water was now itself unclean, having touched the unclean hands, and, if it ran down the fingers again, it would again render them unclean. The process was repeated with the hands held in the opposite direction, with the fingers pointing down; and then finally each hand was cleansed by being rubbed with the fist of the other. A really strict Jew would do all this, not only before a meal, but also between each of the courses.[6]

Jesus responded to this nit-picking, hypocritical rule-keeping—which did more to invalidate the Word of God than to affirm it—with the same hot indignation he expressed in Matthew 23. Feel the righteous anger as you read His words.

> "You hypocrites, rightly did Isaiah prophesy of you, saying,
>> 'This people honors Me with their lips,
>> But their heart is far away from Me.
>> But in vain do they worship Me,
>> Teaching as doctrines the precepts of men.'"
> (Matt. 15:7–9)

Hypocrisy, in whatever form—giving, praying, fasting, empty traditions—touched a raw nerve in Jesus. He didn't just simply frown on it, He attacked it, berated it, and condemned it to a sentence of hell (23:33). Crossroads issue? Absolutely. One that we must all constantly guard against in our struggle to mature as authentic Christians.

---

6. William Barclay, paraphrasing Alfred Edersheim's *The Life and Times of Jesus the Messiah*, in *The Gospel of Matthew*, vol. 2, rev. ed., The Daily Study Bible Series (Philadelphia, Pa.: Westminster Press, 1975), p. 114.

Application: Hypocrisy Opposed

To bring our study to a close, here are three helpful principles to remember. First: *Exposing hypocrisy is helpful.* Especially when it's our own! Are you open to that kind of constructive criticism? If a Paul were to point out flagrant hypocrisy in your life, would you humbly repent? Would you be willing to play the role of a Paul to someone close to you who is playing the role of a *hupokritēs*? And what about your children? Are you helping them discern between what is real Christianity and what's hypocritical religion?

Second: *Practicing hypocrisy is natural.* Hypocrisy isn't just a scribes-and-Pharisees problem; it comes naturally to all of us because we all share the same sin nature. And because it is so innate, it can easily go undetected. Which is why we should be doubly on guard against it.

Third: *Stopping hypocrisy is painful.* It begins with a ruthlessly honest admission of guilt—no excuses, no hedging the extent of the problem, no blaming others. We must not simply frown on our own hypocrisy; we must attack it, berate it, condemn and denounce it with the same vigor Jesus used. It won't be easy, and it may involve some painful decisions and consequences, but it's the only way to free ourselves to begin serving Him again with sincerity of heart and a clear conscience.

> In reference to your former manner of life, you lay aside the old self, which is being corrupted in accordance with the lusts of deceit, and that you be renewed in the spirit of your mind, and put on the new self, which in the likeness of God has been created in righteousness and holiness of the truth. (Eph. 4:22–24)

 Living Insights

STUDY ONE

In his book *Being Holy, Being Human*, Jay Kesler tells this story.

> Phil Donahue, the television talk show host, has something of a reputation for giving clergy a hard time, and he has said the reason he's that way is that he has little respect for them. Most clergy will do anything for some media attention, he says.

In his autobiography, however, he tells about an encounter with a pastor who was different. It happened while Donahue was a young television reporter in Ohio, and one day he was sent to West Virginia to cover a mine disaster. He went by himself in a battered little car, carrying a minicam to film his story.

It was so cold when he got there, however, that the camera wouldn't work. So he put it inside his coat to warm it up enough to run. In the meantime, the families of the trapped miners were gathered around. They were just simple mining people—women, old men, and children. Several of the trapped men were fathers.

Then the local pastor arrived. He was rough-hewn, and he didn't speak well at all. But he gathered all the families around in a circle, and they held one another in their arms while he prayed for them.

As this was going on, Donahue was still trying to get his camera to work, and he was incredibly frustrated because he couldn't film this poignant scene. Finally, after the prayer was over, Donahue managed to get his camera operating. So he told the pastor he had his camera working now and asked if the pastor would please do the prayer again so he could film it for the evening news.

Donahue says, by the way, that he's been with the world's best-known public figures, including preachers, and they're all willing to redo a scene in order to get on the news.

This simple West Virginia preacher, however, told Donahue, "Young man, we don't pray for the news. I'm sorry, but we've already prayed, and I will not pose."

To this day Donahue remembers that pastor with respect. You don't forget that kind of character, no matter who you are or what you believe.[7]

Is there a particular area of your spiritual life where you are posing for praise instead of sincerely seeking God? Sometimes it is

7. Jay Kesler, Being Holy, Being Human (Waco, Tex.: Word Books, 1988), pp. 98–99.

difficult to discern the subtle hypocrisies that have crept into our conduct, but perhaps the following will help. Remember that Jesus condemned the Pharisees in Matthew 23 for two reasons: First, "They say things and do not do them" (v. 3). And second, "They do all their deeds to be noticed by men" (v. 5).

Now ask yourself, "What things am I teaching other Christians or even my own children that I'm not practicing myself?" And then look at the fundamental ways that you practice your righteousness and ask yourself, "What are my motives for doing these things, such as praying, giving, occupying a highly visible position in church, serving on a board, or helping my neighbor? Is it for God's glory, really, or my own?"

_____

_____

_____

_____

🍇 *Living Insights*   STUDY TWO

Besides exposing our own hypocrisy, we need to cultivate the authenticity to replace it. Take some time now to write down what must be done to replace the hypocrisy you uncovered in the first study with genuine faith and conduct.

_____

_____

_____

For help in guarding against the encroachment of hypocrisy in your life, remember these words from Ezra 7:10.

> For Ezra had set his heart to study the law of the
> Lord, and to practice it, and to teach His statutes
> and ordinances in Israel.

Before Ezra attempted to teach God's Word to others, he practiced it. And before he practiced it, he spent time studying it. Study, practice, teach. Set your heart to follow this same pattern, and you will "prove yourselves doers of the word, and not merely hearers who delude themselves" (James 1:22). You'll be authentic.

Chapter 15

THE COMPROMISE OF INTEGRITY

Proverbs 24:10; Psalm 75:5–7; 78:70–72

Integrity is a dying quality in our society. During the past decade, it has languished from neglect in virtually every realm—including God's church. And evidence of its demise among Christians continues to mount at an alarming rate, taking a terrible toll on the respect we once held among the unsaved.

As you study this issue in today's lesson, ask God to guard the integrity of your own heart as well as that of your spiritual leaders. By His grace and power alone, this essential quality can be revived and this trend reversed.

Two Critical Realms of Testing

Adversity is perhaps the most common test of our integrity. Life is laced with hard times—as the book of Job records, "For man is born for trouble, As sparks fly upward" (Job 5:7). And how we respond to trying circumstances reveals the health of our character and the vitality of our integrity.

> If you faint in the day of adversity,
> Your strength is small. (Prov. 24:10 NKJV)

Less common, though possibly more difficult, is the test of prosperity. Scottish essayist Thomas Carlyle once said,

> Adversity is sometimes hard upon a man; but for one man who can stand prosperity, there are a hundred that will stand adversity.[1]

Why? Because few people are able to maintain their spiritual equilibrium when promoted up the ladder of prosperity and popularity. Life gets complicated with prosperity. Often, the higher up

---

This message was not a part of the original series but is compatible with it.

1. Thomas Carlyle, as quoted in *Bartlett's Familiar Quotations*, 15th ed., rev. and enl., ed. Emily Morison Beck (Boston, Mass.: Little, Brown and Co., 1980), p. 474.

we advance, the more responsibilities we assume, the more power and privacy we enjoy, the more hidden autonomy we are given, the more we are tempted to become like King Nebuchadnezzar, who boasted, "Is this not Babylon the great, which I myself have built as a royal residence by the might of my power and for the glory of my majesty?" (Dan. 4:30). And it is extremely difficult for integrity to survive in the thin air of such lofty pride.

The psalmist Asaph conveys God's strong warning:

> "'Do not lift up your horn on high,
> Do not speak with insolent pride.'"
> For not from the east, nor from the west,
> Nor from the desert comes exaltation;
> But God is the Judge;
> He puts down one, and exalts another. (Ps. 75:5–7)

"Lifting up one's horn" is a metaphor from the animal world that signifies arrogance and defiance. Asaph cautions those who are prosperous not to strut proudly as if they were the ones ultimately responsible for their accomplishments. Promotion comes from the sovereign God. Only through humble dependence on Him will our integrity survive the complicated test of being exalted.

Two Clarifying Concepts regarding Leadership

These have been hard days for Christian ministry. The compromise of integrity among our leaders has been epidemic. But we must remember not to let these tragic events cloud our basic understanding of leadership itself. So let's pause briefly to look at two clarifying concepts.

First, *leadership is not wrong*. Success doesn't have to mean disaster. There have been many who kept their balance after being exalted. Like Joseph, for example, who was promoted in one day from prisoner to prime minister over Egypt. And Daniel, who was taken captive to Babylon and later became King Nebuchadnezzar's right-hand man. And Amos, that rugged shepherd whom God promoted to be His prophet at the temple of Bethel. All three men were exalted by God and served with integrity.

Second, *leadership must be accountable*. What do we mean by accountability? Basically, it is this:

> Opening one's life to a few carefully selected, trusted,
> loyal confidants who speak the truth—who have

126

the right to examine, to question, to appraise, and to give counsel. . . . The purpose of the relationship is not to make someone squirm or to pull rank and devastate an individual; no, not at all. Rather, it is to be a helpful sounding board, to guard someone from potential peril, to identify the possibility of a "blind spot," to serve in an advisory capacity, bringing perspective and wisdom where such may be lacking.[2]

Two Crucial Aspects of Leadership

Without the checks and balances of accountability, leaders often develop an unhealthy independence. They become an island to themselves, unapproachable, unquestionable, people whose thoughts and actions are hidden behind the authority and privilege of their position. That can easily lead to a fall spiritually, ethically, or financially. To protect against this all-too-common disaster, the wise leader will heed God's wisdom in Scripture and cultivate this first crucial aspect of accountability.

> Through presumption comes nothing but strife,
> But with those who receive counsel is wisdom.
> (Prov. 13:10)

> The teaching of the wise is a fountain of life,
> To turn aside from the snares of death. (v. 14)

> Poverty and shame will come to him who
>   neglects discipline,
> But he who regards reproof will be honored. (v. 18)

> Iron sharpens iron,
> So one man sharpens another. (27:17)

The second crucial aspect of biblical leadership is integrity. Webster defines it as "an unimpaired condition: soundness. Firm adherence to a code of especially moral or artistic values. Incorruptibility. . . . Synonym: . . . honesty."[3] Another synonym can be found in the picture Psalm 78 paints of David.

2. Charles R. Swindoll, *Living Above the Level of Mediocrity* (Dallas, Tex.: Word Publishing, 1989), pp. 126–27.

3. *Webster's Ninth New Collegiate Dictionary*, see "integrity."

He also chose David His servant,
And took him from the sheepfolds;
From the care of the ewes with suckling lambs He
    brought him,
To shepherd Jacob His people,
And Israel His inheritance.
So he shepherded them according to the integrity
    of his heart,
And guided them with his skillful hands.
(vv. 70–72)

God *chose, took,* and *brought* David to shepherd Israel. He exalted him from tending sheep to shepherding people. But this new flock did not belong to David. These sheep weren't his to manipulate for his own selfish purposes. They belonged to the Lord. So David shepherded the people as God commanded, with skillful hands guided by the integrity of his heart.

In Hebrew, the word for *integrity* used in this passage means "to be complete or finished . . . blameless."

As leaders, it is imperative that we apply self-restraint, that we keep saying no to things that are questionable, that we don't compromise our integrity and bring shame to the cause of Christ.

Some Personal Convictions on Integrity—An Open Letter

To conclude our study on integrity, we want to share with you some excerpts from a letter written by Chuck Swindoll to a friend who asked the timely question, Should leaders who have fallen and repented be allowed back in the spotlight?[4]

Personal Thoughts regarding Hidden Immorality

"Like it or not, accept it or not, we cannot ignore that Scripture does draw a distinction between the common, everyday, all-too-familiar sins in life and the deliberate acting out of sexual sins. This would especially include sexual sins that express themselves in lengthy deception and secret escapades which culminate in scandalous affairs that disrupt entire families . . . corrupting, usually destroying, solid marriages.

---

4. The following material is taken from a "Family Talk on Integrity," given by Charles R. Swindoll at an Insight for Living chapel service, Fullerton, California, May 13, 1987.

"Often, hidden immorality goes on for months, even years, while the one practicing such deeds in private lives a complete lie in public. The sheer shamelessness, insanity, and audacity of it all reveals deep-seated character flaws. Those flaws cause the immoral person involved in the perversion to sin 'against his own body' and thus enter into a unique category of disobedience unlike 'every other sin' [see 1 Cor. 6:18]." . . .

Personal Feelings on the Consequences of Such Hypocrisy

"Severe and tragic consequences follow severe and tragic sins. We have an interesting analogy in our system of jurisprudence. A person guilty of a felony may serve time behind bars, become a model prisoner, acknowledge his or her wrong, and finally be freed, pardoned from the crime of the past. But he or she forfeits the right to vote for the rest of his or her life. . . . That special privilege he or she once enjoyed of participating in our nation's future is forever removed. Once certain sins against one's own body are committed and covered up, later to be discovered, there remains too great a breach in the public's mind to grant that person the full privileges he or she earlier enjoyed. . . . Flawed character breeds distrust." . . .

"Am I suggesting that such shameless and deplorable actions cannot be forgiven? Of course not. But I am admitting that the character flaws which led to those extended and deceptive acts of sensuality may very well restrict such individuals from places of public service they once knew and enjoyed. Not because they haven't confessed and repented. Not because they haven't sincerely claimed Christ's offer of forgiveness. Neither is it because others fail to forgive them. . . . By their 'sinning against their own body,' they reveal a weakness in their moral character which sets in motion certain consequences and many complications. All of this can scandalize the body of Christ if they are brought back before the public to enjoy all the privileges and rights that once were theirs. . . .

"For example, what about the scarred remains of the mate and family members? How do they handle the public adulation granted the one who secretly deceived them, hypocritically abused them, then openly abandoned them for another?" . . .

"It's not a matter of forgiveness, I repeat, but of forfeiting certain rights and privileges. Though God fully forgives, you will recall He kept Moses from the Promised Land, demoted Saul from ruling as king, and restrained David from building the temple. Each was forgiven, yet each was nevertheless divinely restricted from the fulfillment of his dreams.

What about Repentance and Forgiveness?

"Is repentance, then, without value? On the contrary. Without repentance the vertical relationship with God remains hindered and the horizontal relationship with others remains crippled. Furthermore, confession and repentance allow the forgiven to glean God's wisdom from His reproofs and to reestablish a measure of restored harmony with those who were offended in the backwash of that person's sins. Repentance not only validates the sinner's confession, it prompts the offended to fully forgive.

"My problem is not with forgiving, or even with loving a brother or sister who has fallen into the swamp of extensive immorality. I'm often overwhelmed with feelings of compassion for the fallen. My difficulty comes in later promoting that person to a place of respected leadership in the body, the position that requires public trust, credibility of character, the incurring of stricter judgment, and a higher standard of conduct [according to] James 3:1.

"Sins are forgivable, but a weakness of character does not suddenly go away even when one repents. Consequences, though painful, remain. Sinless perfection is not a prerequisite for Christian ministry, but integrity of character is. Hence the requirements listed in 1 Timothy 3:

> An overseer, then, must be above reproach, the husband of one wife, temperate, prudent, respectable. . . . He must have a good reputation with those outside the church. (vv. 2, 7a)

The Necessity of a Contrite Heart

". . . The forgiven sinner of today is often one who expects, dare I say, *demands*, more than he or she should. Scripture calls this presumption. A broken and contrite heart is not presumptuous; it makes no demands, entertains no expectations.

"I've noticed that those recovering from a sexual scandal sometimes judge rather harshly others who are reluctant to allow them all the leadership they once exercised. I've often heard them refer to this as 'shooting our wounded,' when in fact those most wounded are the people who trusted when the fallen leader was living a lie. My question is, Who's shooting whom? A presumptuous spirit usually reveals itself in an aggressive desire to return to a platform of public ministry. When that desire isn't granted, those being restrained can easily present themselves as pathetic, helpless victims of others' judgment and condemnation. I find that response manipulative and not a little bit disturbing.

"What concerns me most about this whole scenario is an absence of abject submission to God and utter humility before others. . . . The truly repentant soul, it seems to me, should be so overwhelmed by humiliation and so grateful for the grace of God, he or she has no room for fawning pride within or frowning accusation without."

As we conclude our study on integrity, a final fact emerges: But for the grace and mercy of God, we could all be guilty of the worst of sins. Personal purity is never automatic or easy. Integrity doesn't develop without effort. Both must be cultivated and guarded each day. May these words be used not as a stone to throw at someone else, but as a warning for ourselves lest we, too, compromise our integrity.

 ## *Living Insights*   STUDY ONE

Quite often today, it is sexual immorality that casts a shadow on the integrity of Christians. And though we may like to believe that it only happens to a few on the fringe, in reality there are many in the mainstream who are struggling in this area. If you are one of these secret strugglers, this Living Insight is for you.

◆

Sexual immorality, an addiction to pornography . . . how did it happen? When did it begin? Perhaps you can remember a specific time or event, perhaps not. The fact is, you're caught up in some form of sexual immorality and have not been able to overcome it. Oh, you've tried, you've confessed it to God; but you keep going back to it, and have been doing so for years.

You're not some crazed-looking fiend, however. You haven't run off and left your family or denied your faith. Quite the opposite. You've tried to grow, tried to lead a faithful and responsible life. And in the midst of all this you have gradually taken on bigger and bigger responsibilities. Someone asked you to lead the worship songs, teach a Bible study, serve as a deaconess or elder, or pastor a church. Your first reaction was to say no. The guilt of your hidden sin was too much. It would be too hypocritical. But then you thought, "I'm going to quit. This is it, I'll stop." So you confessed the sin, asked for God's strength to stay pure, and took the position offered.

For a while you did stop, and it seemed that you had overcome the addiction; but then it started all over again—the sin, the lies, the covering up. You felt guilty and wanted to confess, but the terror of revealing this sin and facing all its horrible ramifications drove you to rationalize instead. "There's no need to bring it up, I'm going to quit. That's the last time I'll ever do that."

But of course it wasn't. You're still addicted. And your life has become a living hell, a house divided against itself. You want to serve Christ, but you cannot escape the bondage to this other master. Now, today, years since this all began, you're wondering, "How can I confess this? Who will love me when I tell them I'm addicted to pornography or have been a child molester or have been involved in homosexuality? I'll lose everything—friends, family, position, privileges. What can I do?"

◆

There is no easy way to regain your integrity after living a lie for years. The truth is, it will be a painful process to expose this sinful part of your private life. But it's better to do what is right and suffer for it than to continue living a life of hypocrisy and deception (1 Pet. 2:20). The one pain will lead to healing, the other only to deeper misery and trouble for you and many others.

If you're tired of carrying this tremendous burden, if you're sick of being a hypocrite and want to break free of this bondage, pray for God to guide you to someone whose spiritual maturity you respect. Perhaps a pastor, or counselor—someone who has experience in helping broken people seek restoration. Then take a step of faith and confess your secret to this person. Will you take time to begin praying for this person now?

 ## Living Insights

As we saw in our lesson, integrity's greatest safeguard is probably *accountability*. Accountability requires at least four things from us:

- *Vulnerability*—capable of being wounded, shown to be wrong, even admitting it before being confronted.

- *Teachability*—a willingness to learn, being quick to hear and respond to reproof, being open to counsel.

- *Availability*—accessible, touchable, able to be interrupted.

- *Honesty*—committed to the truth regardless of how much it hurts, a willingness to admit the truth no matter how difficult or humiliating the admission may be. Hating all that is phony or false.[5]

How present are these qualities in your life? Don't quickly dismiss this question—stop, take time to search your soul for the answer. What do you find?

Vulnerability _____

_____

Teachability _____

_____

Availability _____

_____

Honesty _____

_____

These qualities comprise and ensure integrity—a character trait *essential* to your walk with God.

> O Lord, who may abide in Thy tent?
> Who may dwell on Thy holy hill?
> He who walks with integrity, and works righteous-
>   ness,
> And speaks truth in his heart.
> (Ps. 15:1–2)

5. Swindoll, *Mediocrity*, p. 127.

Chapter 16

CHRIST AT THE CROSSROAD OF DISQUALIFICATION

1 Corinthians 9:24–10:13

Disqualified. The mere mention of the word stirs up strong emotions. It smacks of shame, humiliation, the worst kind of failure. Whether one is disqualified from serving in the military or the government, or from practicing law or medicine makes no difference. And for Christians who are disqualified because of flagrant sin, there are additional ruinous results.[1] We lose the opportunity to serve as godly role models. We spiritually devastate those who had placed their trust in us. And worst of all, we cause "the name of God and our doctrine" to be spoken against, ridiculed (1 Tim. 6:1).

Today we want to walk through a serious section of Scripture— the last four verses of 1 Corinthians 9 and the first thirteen verses of chapter 10—and read words that probe deeply, words of warning that we dare not take lightly. As we study these penetrating words, open your heart to the Spirit of God, who will teach, reprove, expose, and hopefully encourage you with the reminder that Christ meets us even at the crossroad of disqualification.

Scriptural Word Pictures regarding Distinctives

In a previous lesson, Christ's counsel concerning hypocrites was simple and straightforward—"Do not be like them" (Matt. 6:8). For unless we are different from them, we, too, will be disqualified and lose our effectiveness as Christians. What are we to be like, then?

We're to Be Salt, Light, and Stars

We're to be "salt" (Matt. 5:13)—people who create a thirst for God in others by the way we live, people whose lives work as a preservative for good and as a protection against evil. We're also to be "light" that illuminates the truth and gives direction (v. 14).

---

1. By disqualification we do *not* mean a believer loses his or her salvation. Rather, because of flagrant sin, a Christian may be disqualified from a role of authority, respect, liberties, privileges, all of which were built on trust. The loss of these things is not necessarily permanent; some or all may be regained in time.

And we're to shine like stars by modeling the luminescent character of Christ against the dark background of "a crooked and perverse generation" (Phil. 2:14–15).

We're to Condition and Control Our Bodies

In 1 Corinthians 9, the apostle Paul gives us yet another important word picture to ponder. One that not only depicts what we're to be like but also reminds us that it takes a great deal of discipline, self-control, and determination to be an effective Christian.

> Do you not know that those who run in a race all run, but only one receives the prize? Run in such a way that you may win. And everyone who competes in the games exercises self-control in all things. They then do it to receive a perishable wreath, but we an imperishable. (vv. 24–25)

William Barclay gives us further insight into the relevance of this image to Paul and his readers.

> [Paul] insists to those Corinthians who wanted to take the easy way that no man will ever get anywhere without the sternest self-discipline. Paul was always fascinated by the picture of the athlete. An athlete must train with intensity if he is to win his contest; and Corinth knew how thrilling contests could be, for at Corinth the Isthmian games, second only to the Olympic games, were held. Furthermore, the athlete undergoes this self-discipline and this training to win a crown of laurel leaves that within days will be a withered chaplet. How much more should the Christian discipline himself to win the crown which is eternal life.[2]

With this imperishable, eternal crown in view, Paul describes the rigorous spiritual training he was undergoing to stay in the race as a qualified messenger of God.

> Therefore I run in such a way, as not without aim; I box in such a way, as not beating the air; but I buffet my body and make it my slave. (vv. 26–27a)

2. William Barclay, *The Letters to the Corinthians*, rev. ed., The Daily Study Bible Series (Philadelphia, Pa.: Westminster Press, 1975), p. 85.

Paul didn't have an ounce of fat on him, spiritually speaking. Everything he did was designed to strengthen his godly character and keep his witness well toned. For his one overriding concern was that

> lest possibly, after I have preached to others, I myself should be disqualified. (v. 27b)

Personal Warnings regarding Disqualification

The apostle Paul, disqualified? The thought seems incredible, yet he clearly had a wholesome fear of compromising his calling. This fear didn't come so much from his exposure to the world but from his *overexposure* to spiritual things. For he knew—and this is why he wrote this warning to fellow believers, fellow traffickers in truth—that familiarity with the spiritual can breed indifference and contempt, rather than fostering intimacy and devotion.

The Silent Perils of Overexposure

With the ink still wet on verse 27, there suddenly flashed into the Apostle's mind a classic example of overexposure leading to disqualification.[3] As we follow Paul's line of reasoning, pay particular attention to his repeated use of the word *all*.

> For I do not want you to be unaware, brethren, that our fathers were all under the cloud, and all passed through the sea; and all were baptized into Moses in the cloud and in the sea; and all ate the same spiritual food; and all drank the same spiritual drink, for they were drinking from a spiritual rock which followed them; and the rock was Christ. (10:1–4)

Paul is reminding his readers of the Israelites, who had everything during the Exodus. They all followed the cloud which gave them supernatural guidance. They all passed through the Red Sea by supernatural deliverance. They all were shepherded by Moses, who provided supernatural leadership. And they all feasted on the

---

3. As we continue reading through chapter 10, we must remember that when Paul wrote this letter to the Corinthians, he didn't break down his thoughts into verses and chapters; rather, his thoughts flowed together. So there really is no break between his last thought in 9:27 and his next in 10:1.

same supernatural diet. Surely, with such unparalleled nearness to God's presence and power, those people most of all would have pleased Him. Wrong.

> Nevertheless, with most of them God was not well-pleased; for they were laid low in the wilderness. (v. 5)

Instead of being thankful for God's supernatural provisions, the Hebrews developed an attitude of ingratitude, which later resulted in rebellion. Those highly privileged people became a disqualified people, just as a highly gifted yet overconfident athlete can become a washout.

Now Paul didn't review this simply that we might be good students of Jewish history. He had a purpose. Jump ahead for a moment to verse 11.

> Now these things happened to them as an example,
> and they were written for our instruction. (v. 11a)

In Greek, the word for *example* used here and in verse 6 is *tupos*, which means "an impression, the mark of a blow,"[4] like the stamp of a die. Paul wants the *tupos* of those Israelites to make a deep impression in our hearts so that we will not be like them. And that's exactly why Jesus warned us not to be like the scribes and Pharisees. For they, too, became insensitive to God and, later, smug in the self-righteousness they derived from their own religiosity.

The Subtle Temptations of Cynicism

Going back to verse 6, we see Paul describing what in particular caused those people to become disqualified, although they had known God's blessing and presence so well.[5] First, it started with an inner attitude.

> We should not crave evil things, as they also craved.
> (v. 6b)

Though it may seem hard to believe, it was in the midst of that miraculous Exodus—when God's holy presence was constantly before them—that the Israelites lusted after things that were evil. And

---

4. W. E. Vine, *Vine's Expository Dictionary of New Testament Words* (McLean, Va.: MacDonald Publishing Co., n.d.), p. 373.

5. The scenes Paul will be referring to in 1 Corinthians 10:6–10 are found in Numbers 11; Exodus 32, particularly verse 6; Numbers 25; Numbers 21:4–9; and Numbers 16.

not just one or two people, but most of them! These secret cravings later blossomed into something bigger—idolatry.

> And do not be idolaters as some of them were. . . .
> (v. 7a)

Idolatry means dethroning Christ and enthroning someone or something else as the focus of our thoughts and affection. Like evil cravings, this also takes place in the secrecy of the heart, makes no noise, and attracts little or no attention. But if left unchecked, it will eventually erode our faith until all pretenses of godliness collapse and we're swept away into flagrant immorality.

> Nor let us act immorally, as some of them did, and twenty-three thousand fell in one day. (v. 8)

The word *immorally* here comes from the Greek term *pornos*, which means "fornication." Sexual immorality became rampant in the time of the Exodus, just as it was in first-century Corinth and is today. Next, Paul notes how they took God's grace for granted.

> Nor let us try the Lord, as some of them did, and were destroyed by the serpents. (v. 9)

Despite God's goodness toward them, the people bitterly complained against His plans and provisions. They arrogantly presumed upon His patience and long-suffering and paid dearly for it. Still, the lesson of the serpents didn't keep them from grumbling.

> Nor grumble, as some of them did, and were destroyed by the destroyer. (v. 10)

The tongue tells the story of the heart. And the heart that was revealed on the lips of those Israelites was often bitter and profane.

Though the moment of their fall may have been sudden and disastrous, it had a long past that went all the way back to evil cravings that had not been dealt with. Remember that these people weren't simply some ungodly group roaming around in the wilderness; they were God's chosen people! But they didn't protect themselves from the dangers of overexposure, and they lost everything: their wonder of the miraculous, their awe of the unusual, their fear of God, and their effectiveness as His representatives. Instead of being salt and light to a lost world, they became only dust for the desert.

Dual Reactions regarding Defeat

The disqualification of millions of privileged people is a sobering example to us all. And for those who are tempted to think, "That will never happen to me," Paul cautions,

> Therefore let him who thinks he stands take heed lest he fall. (v. 12)

There is no guarantee that we will never fail or be disqualified. Effective, authentic Christianity is something that must be cultivated and maintained every day.

On the other hand, for those who feel, "I'm too far gone, there's no hope, I can't recover," the Apostle offers this encouragement.

> No temptation has overtaken you but such as is common to man; and God is faithful, who will not allow you to be tempted beyond what you are able, but with the temptation will provide the way of escape also, that you may be able to endure it. (v. 13)

To close our study, let's consider how close to the crossroad of disqualification we may be with these four probing questions.

- Have you maintained your commitment to the Lord, or has it begun to fade?

- If your walk with Christ has slipped, can you locate when or where the spiritual erosion began to occur?

- Do you realize the danger of continuing in your present course?

- Are you aware of the devastating impact you will have on your family and friends if you fall?

Are you dangerously close to being disqualified? Has your Christianity lost its ability to create a thirst for God in others, to illuminate the truth and give direction? Regardless of how unfaithful you may have been, Christ is faithful to forgive and to provide a way of escape so that you can endure, regaining the brilliance of His life in you.

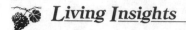

Living Insights

Another tragic biblical example of disqualification is Samson. Like the Hebrews of the Exodus, he, too, was highly privileged with God's miraculous blessings. And he, too, reached the point where he didn't take God or His blessings seriously.

Go back and read Samson's story in Judges 13:2–5, 24 and chapters 14–16. Then see if you can identify some of the same mistakes in Samson's life that we discovered in the Israelites.

• The very real dangers for those of us who claim the name of Christ begin as unseen cravings, spawned in secrecy, pampered in private. From reading Samson's story, what particular inner attitude do you feel contributed to his downfall?

_____

_____

• Samson was "a Nazarite to God from the womb" (Judg. 13:5); his life was to be totally consecrated to God. But was it? Did Samson sacrifice all to please God? Or was his worship and devotion to Jehovah eroded by a devotion to someone or something else? If so, what was it, and when do you see it happening?

_____

_____

• When did Samson get caught up in the sin of *pornos?* Was there any indication of repentance?

_____

_____

• Like the children of Israel in the wilderness, Samson took advantage of God's grace and presumed upon His patience. He played with something that should have been kept a holy secret. Can you think of when and how he did this?

_____

_____

_____

- As judge of all Israel for twenty-plus years, how do you think Samson's life impacted that nation? What about Israel's enemies? Without his miraculous strength, would there have been any noticeable witness for the Lord about his life, as it is described in the Scriptures?

_____

_____

_____

_____

- And last, consider how much more God could have accomplished through Samson had he lived a long life of obedience instead of straying and sacrificing his life to kill only a few thousand enemies.

 ## *Living Insights*

Are you winded spiritually? Have you pushed yourself too hard to grow too fast? You may have reached your spiritual breaking point. Your heart and mind can't take anymore. They need rest, time to assimilate the truth, time to rebuild. But many of us never give ourselves that time. We race from one meeting, Bible study, or church function to the next, never slowing down, until one day we collapse in exhaustion—or worse, we fall and become disqualified.

- Are you a youth leader who's so busy that your only time in God's Word is spent in hasty, last-minute preparations for Bible studies?

- Are you a pastor who can't read or hear God's Word without critiquing how you can use it in your next sermon?

- Are you a Christian leader who's so busy that prayer has become only a perfunctory public performance?

- Spiritually, do you feel like you're always two steps behind? And only one step ahead of disaster?

If this describes you, you need rest. You need to cut back on all the Christian activities and rehabilitate your own spiritual vitality. Avoid the crossroad of disqualification by reestablishing a realistic spiritual workout schedule for yourself. Get back to the basics, such as prayer, personal Bible study, meditation, and solitude. Then look at your schedule and pace yourself with regard to the number of Bible studies you will attend and lead. Use the space provided to chart any needed changes, and remember, the Christian faith is a marathon, not a one-hundred-yard dash. Adjust your schedule and run to win!

Spiritual Workout Schedule							
	Mon.	Tues.	Wed.	Thurs.	Fri.	Sat.	Sun.
Prayer							
Bible Study (Personal)							
(With a Group)							
(As a Leader)							
Meditation							
Solitude							

Chapter 17

CHRIST AT THE CROSSROAD OF INADEQUACY

Matthew 28:16–20; Acts 1:4–5, 8

Inadequacy—a daunting crossroad. One that many of us never seem to get past our whole lives. We get stuck in the quicksand of our own feelings of weakness; and though some days we almost free ourselves of them, we inevitably slide right back, sucked in by vague, unrelenting thoughts and feelings that would bury our sense of value.

All of us have struggled against inadequacy's downward pull into nothingness. Sometimes we've felt inadequate to overcome a long-standing habit or addiction, do a particular job, face a surgery that could mean the beginning of the end, stay in a marriage that is unfulfilling, live with a disability for the rest of our lives . . . the list has no end. The dark abyss of inadequate feelings has no bottom. And many of us have sunk deep into its despairing grip.

The Inescapable Fact of Human Inadequacy

Our sense of inadequacy is inextricably bound to our very identity as frail and fallible human beings. It feeds, like a parasite, on our shortcomings. It thrives on our natural infirmities, constantly humbling us, continually pushing us down for simply being human.

What It Means

Perhaps our understanding of this crossroads issue would be enhanced if we defined it by first looking at its opposite. According to Webster, the word *adequate* means "sufficient for a specific requirement."[1] The idea is being capable or qualified. *Inadequate*, therefore, means *insufficient, incapable, unable.*

Why It's True

Why does God allow us to stumble along our insufficient, incapable, unable way? So that we might become convinced that our

---

1. *Webster's Ninth New Collegiate Dictionary,* see "adequate."

adequacy is from Him. The apostle Paul certainly became convinced. For when he contemplated the eternal consequences of his ministry, he felt totally inadequate.

> For we are a fragrance of Christ to God among those who are being saved and among those who are perishing; to the one an aroma from death to death, to the other an aroma from life to life. And who is adequate for these things? (2 Cor. 2:15–16)

Who is inherently capable to handle such an incredible responsibility? No one. So where did Paul's adequacy come from to do the things he did?

> Not that we are adequate in ourselves to consider anything as coming from ourselves, but our adequacy is from God. (3:5)

With genuine humility, Paul attributed his competence in ministry wholly to God. His confidence soared because of God's divine power, but never so high that he lost sight of the sobering reality of his inadequacy without Him.

The Unparalleled Challenge of Jesus' Commission

Like Paul, the disciples were also keenly aware of their own inadequacy—particularly after being with Jesus for three years and then deserting Him at His arrest. And yet, a little over a month after His resurrection, Christ commissioned those same timid men to make disciples of all the nations. No group ever had a greater challenge, and at the same time, no group ever had a greater reason to feel inadequate.

Let's go back and discover what transformed these unschooled and unsophisticated followers into powerful witnesses, able to fulfill a commission that was humanly impossible.

A Study in Contrasts

Following His resurrection, Jesus told His disciples to meet Him in Galilee. So

> the eleven disciples proceeded to Galilee, to the mountain which Jesus had designated. And when they saw Him, they worshiped Him; but some were doubtful. (Matt. 28:16–17)

Consider the contrast between the disciples and Jesus on that mountain. On the one hand, you have a small band of frightened, doubting disciples; on the other is the all-powerful, resurrected Savior. They were only human—limited, unsure, moody, shortsighted. Inadequate followers, not leaders. He was God's Son, omniscient and omnipotent. These were men who for the past three years had mainly witnessed miracles, not performed them. They didn't multiply the loaves and fishes for the thousands, they simply passed them out. They didn't still the wind and the waves, they simply watched. Jesus had always been the one who wielded the power and led. But all that was about to change.

A Command and a Promise

> And Jesus came up and spoke to them, saying, "All authority has been given to Me in heaven and on earth." (v. 18)

Considering how dismayed the disciples had been by the Crucifixion, they were undoubtedly glad to hear Jesus say this. His next words, however, probably caused more feelings of inadequacy than joy.

> "Go therefore and make disciples of all the nations, baptizing them in the name of the Father and the Son and the Holy Spirit, teaching them to observe all that I commanded you." (vv. 19–20a)

The Great Commission, as this is called, actually has only one command—"make disciples of all the nations." To accomplish this task, however, Jesus instructed the disciples to leave the familiar— "go"; to identify new converts as His followers by "baptizing"; and to feed them His Word by "teaching." But as much as their hearts burned to obey their Savior, they could not escape the feeling that these commands were beyond their human power. And even Jesus' next promise, words of timeless comfort, couldn't completely erase their sense of inadequacy.

> "And lo, I am with you always, even to the end of the age." (v. 20b)

The disciples probably knew that to succeed they needed more than the *company* of Someone who had all authority in heaven and earth. They needed a *transition*, a transfer of His authority to themselves. For only then could the humanly impossible become possible. And Jesus knew this too.

The Unique Transition of Divine Authority

Picking up where Matthew's gospel left off is the book of Acts. Here we will see that Jesus did more than promise the disciples His presence. He also promised a desperately needed transfusion of power. Beginning in chapter 1, Luke records Jesus' final words to the disciples before the epochal moment of His ascension into heaven.

> And gathering them together, He commanded them not to leave Jerusalem, but to wait for what the Father had promised, "Which," He said, "you heard of from Me; for John baptized with water, but you shall be baptized with the Holy Spirit not many days from now. . . . You shall receive power when the Holy Spirit has come upon you; and you shall be My witnesses both in Jerusalem, and in all Judea and Samaria, and even to the remotest part of the earth." (vv. 4–5, 8)

The disciples were going to receive the Holy Spirit's gift of power, the same power they had seen working in Jesus. A power strong enough to transform them into bold, sufficient, capable witnesses, even to the remotest part of the earth!

A. B. Bruce, in his book *The Training of the Twelve*, expanded on what that power meant.

> All that the apostles were to gain from the mission of the Comforter—enlightenment of mind, enlargement of heart, sanctification of their faculties, and transformation of their characters, so as to make them whetted swords . . . for subduing the world unto the truth; these, or the effect of these combined, constituted the power for which Jesus directed the eleven to wait. . . .
> . . . It was evidently indispensable to success. . . . The world is to be evangelized, not by men invested with ecclesiastical dignities and with parti-colored garments, but by men who have experienced the baptism of the Holy Ghost, and who are visibly endued with the divine power of wisdom, and love, and zeal. As the promised power was indispensable, so it was in its nature a thing simply to be waited for. The disciples were directed to tarry till it came.

They were [not] to attempt to do without it . . .
They fully understood that the power was needful,
and that it could not be [humanly induced], but must
come down.[2]

And indeed it did. Acts 2 records the amazing events that took place on the day of Pentecost when the Spirit descended, the disciples were empowered, and the church began.

And so . . .

Meeting Christ at the crossroad of inadequacy is difficult for most of us because it goes completely against our nature to admit our weaknesses. We may know the truth of them deep inside, but our pride often prevents us from seeking help when we need it. And so we stumble along our insufficient, incapable, and unable way, making terrible mistakes with tragic consequences. Much of this can be avoided, however, if we will remember to earnestly put into practice the following two thoughts from our study.

First, *admitting your inadequacies is the initial step toward accepting God's solution.* No one has ever been helped who refused to admit there is a problem. Don't let your pride blind you to making the same mistakes over and over again. Rather, confess your weaknesses to Christ, and remember these encouraging words from the apostle Paul.

> And He has said to me, "My grace is sufficient for you, for power is perfected in weakness." Most gladly, therefore, I will rather boast about my weaknesses, that the power of Christ may dwell in me. Therefore I am well content with weaknesses, with insults, with distresses, with persecutions, with difficulties, for Christ's sake; for when I am weak, then I am strong. (2 Cor. 12:9–10)

Second, *claiming Christ's power is the ultimate secret of living above the drag of our humanity.* He knows we are inadequate to handle temptation, pain, death, and all the other crossroads we've discussed in this series. And He's willing to strengthen us with the grace we need to be adequate, to mature, and to be His witnesses even to the remotest part of the earth. Are you willing to depend on Him for that power?

2. A. B. Bruce, *The Training of the Twelve*, 4th ed., rev. (1894; reprint, Grand Rapids, Mich.: Kregel Publications, 1971), pp. 536–37.

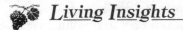

Many of us struggle with dark feelings of inadequacy. They grip us in a nightmarish struggle that ever pulls us toward the brink of nothingness. A state that often results in our feeling too unworthy to pray, too depressed to read God's Word, too timid to share Christ with others, too worthless to do much of anything.

Does this describe you? Are your feelings of inadequacy driving you away from Jesus rather than to Him? Take a moment to meditate on these words from Jesus in John 15 and, as you do, honestly evaluate your present spiritual condition.

> "Abide in Me, and I in you. As the branch cannot bear fruit of itself, unless it abides in the vine, so neither can you, unless you abide in Me. I am the vine, you are the branches; he who abides in Me, and I in him, he bears much fruit; for apart from Me you can do nothing." (vv. 4–5)

Bible Study _____

Prayer _____

Meditation _____

Fellowship _____

Worship _____

Personal Disciplines _____

_____

"For apart from Me you can do *nothing*" (emphasis added). That is the kind of nothingness every believer fears most. A spiritually dry and fruitless life because we've allowed our inadequacies to hinder our dependence on the Vine.

If you have withdrawn from Him whose power is perfected in weakness, take some time now to abide in Christ through prayer. Confess to Him your weaknesses. Unburden your heart of those fears and anxieties. Trust in Him to strengthen you. And as you go forth, cultivate this attitude in yourself which was also in Paul, "Most gladly, therefore, I will rather boast about my weaknesses, that the power of Christ may dwell in me" (2 Cor. 12:9b).

In addition to withdrawing from Christ, is there a particular task your feelings of inadequacy cause you to shy away from? For example, are you hesitant about sharing Christ with others? Do you have some really good thoughts you'd like to express and don't feel able to speak in front of a group? Give this some thought and write down one particular area of insecurity.

_____

_____

_____

_____

One of the ways we learn to depend on Jesus to perfect His power in our weakness is through the support of other believers (Matt. 18:20; Gal. 6:2; Rom. 12:4–13). They can encourage us through prayer, accountability, understanding, biblical instruction, and numerous other ways.

Is there someone you respect spiritually with whom you could share the specific inadequacy you identified? In what ways do you think they could best minister to you?

_____

_____

_____

_____

_____

Last, if you're serious about this, arrange now to see this person at the soonest possible time.

Chapter 18

GOD'S SON:
ALL THROUGH THE BOOK

Luke 24:13–48

"Y ou can't see the forest for the trees." We have often used that
old expression to describe the difficulty of getting above the
details to get a grasp of the bigger picture. But it can also be used
to describe the problem most of us have with the Bible.

Many Christians are familiar with the doctrines woven through
the fabric of the Scriptures, and others know the great Bible stories
and characters—some of whom we've met in our crossroads study.
But we often fail to grasp the fundamental theme of the Bible:
Christ throughout God's Word.

Let's do that in this lesson. Let's meet Him in both the Old
and the New Testaments, see His presence as it is clearly set forth
from Genesis through the Revelation. To start our journey, let's join
Jesus on the Emmaus road as He explains to two weary and dis-
heartened disciples "the things concerning Himself in all the Scriptures" (Luke 24:27).

The Emmaus Experience

It had been a horrid, agonizing week. The One they had pinned
all their hopes and dreams on, Jesus, had been arrested, falsely
accused, beaten, and—unbelievably—crucified. They thought they
had reached the end of the road when the stone was rolled into
place over the opening of the tomb . . . until word came three days
later that the grave was empty and Jesus was alive! How many more
jolts could a disciple take? Discouraged and confused, two of them
turned for home. But the road home was hardly the end; it was just
the beginning.

Disciples in the Dark

And behold, two of them were going that very
day to a village named Emmaus, which was about
seven miles from Jerusalem. And they were convers-

This message was not a part of the original series but is compatible with it.

150

ing with each other about all these things which had taken place. And it came about that while they were conversing and discussing, Jesus Himself approached, and began traveling with them. But their eyes were prevented from recognizing Him. (Luke 24:13–16)

In His post-resurrection body, Jesus is traveling incognito, so to speak. He is able to appear and vanish, move through space with no restraints at all. And He has a ripe opportunity to probe two of His followers concerning the meaning of His death and resurrection. So He asks them,

"What are these words that you are exchanging with one another as you are walking?" (v. 17)

Shocked that someone could be so near Jerusalem and not know what has happened, they sadly relate the week's events (vv. 18–24). As they talk, Jesus perceives a mixture of disappointment, doubt, and confusion in their words. So He decides that it's time to enlighten their darkened spirits.

Christ Brings the Light

"O foolish men and slow of heart to believe in all that the prophets have spoken! Was it not necessary for the Christ to suffer these things and to enter into His glory?" And beginning with Moses and with all the prophets, He explained to them the things concerning Himself in *all* the Scriptures. (vv. 25–27, emphasis added)

What a great moment. . . . Christ teaches the Scriptures.

Notice the word "explained" in verse 27. From its Greek root we get our word *hermeneutics*, which refers to the principles or study of biblical interpretation. In other words, Jesus went back to the books of Moses, Genesis through Deuteronomy, through all of the prophets, ending with Malachi, and interpreted them for these two disciples. He showed them the truth about Himself—the main theme—in all of Scripture.

How wonderful to have God Himself explaining His Word to you! Though they didn't yet know who this wise Man was, when these disciples finally reach Emmaus, they understandably want Him to stay with them. And are they in for a surprise.

151

> And they approached the village where they were
> going, and He acted as though He would go farther.
> And they urged Him, saying, "Stay with us, for it is
> getting toward evening, and the day is now nearly
> over." And He went in to stay with them. And it
> came about that when He had reclined at the table
> with them, He took the bread and blessed it, and
> breaking it, He began giving it to them. And their
> eyes were opened and they recognized Him; and He
> vanished from their sight. (vv. 28–31)

Imagine their astonishment as, at once, their eyes widen, "You're
Je—" and blink—He disappears!

> And they said to one another, "Were not our hearts
> burning within us while He was speaking to us on
> the road, while He was explaining the Scriptures to
> us?" (v. 32)

This "explaining" has a different meaning from "explained" in
verse 27. Here it means "open," the same as their eyes were "opened"
in verse 31. The implication is this: Scripture is incomprehensible
until we see the illuminating truth of Jesus, its major theme. It's
like trying to put together a puzzle with no picture, like trying to
pilot a plane with no map. Without seeing Christ in the Bible, we
travel blindly through a maze of meaningless ideas and people and
events. For He is the key that, when turned correctly, unlocks the
truth and opens eternal mysteries for us.

The two men cannot wait until morning to share their experience with the other disciples. So they run back to Jerusalem, and,
half gasping for breath and half laughing with joy, they relate the
day's startling events, saying, "The Lord has really risen" (vv. 33–35)!

But the Lord has one more dramatic surprise in store for His
disciples.

> And while they were telling these things, He
> Himself stood in their midst. But they were startled
> and frightened and thought that they were seeing a
> spirit. And He said to them, "Why are you troubled,
> and why do doubts arise in your hearts? See My
> hands and My feet, that it is I Myself; touch Me
> and see, for a spirit does not have flesh and bones
> as you see that I have." (vv. 36–39)

Christ proves He is no ghost by letting the disciples touch Him. Then He even eats a piece of fish, showing them, once and for all, that He is really alive (vv. 40–43).[1] Having their full attention now, He turns again to the Scriptures to explain Himself and His death and resurrection.

> Now He said to them, "These are My words which I spoke to you while I was still with you, that all things which are written about Me in the Law of Moses and the Prophets and the Psalms must be fulfilled." Then He opened their minds to understand the Scriptures, and He said to them, "Thus it is written, that the Christ should suffer and rise again from the dead the third day; and that repentance for forgiveness of sins should be proclaimed in His name to all the nations, beginning from Jerusalem. You are witnesses of these things." (vv. 44–48)

When Christ opens the minds of the disciples, they see, for the first time, what the Scriptures are all about. You can imagine their responses as lights go on all over the room. "Yes!" "Of course!" "Why didn't we see that before?" "Now I understand!"

One of the disciples in the room that night later became a courageous witness. Standing before the people who had shouted to crucify Jesus, he proclaims his new understanding of the Scripture's true meaning.

Opened Minds Can Open Hearts

> "The God of Abraham, Isaac, and Jacob, the God of our fathers, has glorified His servant Jesus, the one whom you delivered up, and disowned in the presence of Pilate, when he had decided to release Him. . . . And now, brethren, I know that you acted in ignorance, just as your rulers did also. But the things which God announced beforehand *by the mouth of all the prophets*, that His Christ should suffer, He has thus fulfilled. Repent therefore and return, that your sins may be wiped away, in order that times of refreshing may come from the presence of the Lord." (Acts 3:13, 17–19, emphasis added)

1. Jesus' resurrected body is an archetype of what our own resurrected bodies will be like (see 1 John 3:2).

Then, later, this same dauntless disciple testified again,

> "You know of Jesus of Nazareth, how God anointed Him with the Holy Spirit and with power. . . . And [Jesus] ordered us to preach to the people, and solemnly to testify that this is the One who has been appointed by God as Judge of the living and the dead. *Of Him all the prophets bear witness* that through His name everyone who believes in Him receives forgiveness of sins." (10:38a, 42–43, emphasis added)

Who is this man who is so strong in his faith?

Peter.

Peter? The one who, only weeks before, forsook his Lord and denied that he even knew Him?

The same.

What changed Peter's heart of fear into one of courage?

The understanding he was given by Jesus of the Scriptures transformed his life. The Spirit of the living God, coupled with the understanding of the Word of God, turned Peter, once fearful and denying, into a rock of stability and unintimidated courage!

Our Experience

In order for us to have a faith that matches Peter's, our understanding of Scripture will need to be strong and clear. We, too, will need to grasp the central theme of Christ throughout all of God's Word.

Christ All through Our Bibles

Allow the following chart to acquaint you with Christ throughout the Bible.

Books of the Bible	Names of Christ
Genesis	Seed of the Woman
Exodus	Passover Lamb
Leviticus	Atoning Sacrifice
Numbers	Bronze Serpent
Deuteronomy	Promised Prophet
Joshua	Unseen Captain
Judges	Our Deliverer
Ruth	Our Heavenly Kinsman

1 and 2 Samuel,	Promised King
1 and 2 Kings,	
1 and 2 Chronicles	
Ezra and Nehemiah	Restorer of the Nation
Esther	Our Advocate
Job	Our Redeemer
Psalms	Our All in All
Proverbs	Our Pattern
Ecclesiastes	Our Goal
Song of Solomon	Our Beloved
All the Prophets	Coming Prince of Peace
Matthew	Christ, the King
Mark	Christ, the Servant
Luke	Christ, the Son of Man
John	Christ, the Son of God
Acts	Christ Ascended, Seated, Sending
All the Letters	Christ Indwelling, Filling
Revelation	Christ Returning, Reigning

But there's more!

In the thirty-nine Old Testament books, Christ is in the shadows, seen in analogies and in pictures. He is in types and rituals. He is prophesied and anticipated. The twenty-seven New Testament books complete the Old, revealing Christ in person, in truth and reality, in the present and acknowledged.[2]

Christ within Our Hearts

If you follow the trail of Christ through the Bible and through life, you will come to a clearing at the end in which all else dissolves in the blinding light of Jesus Himself. The apostle John has given us a preview of coming attractions.

> And I saw heaven opened; and behold, a white horse, and He who sat upon it is called Faithful and

---

2. Perhaps like those two disciples on the road to Emmaus, your eyes have never been opened to the main theme of the Bible. If you would like help in seeing Christ all throughout the Scriptures, here are some helpful resources: Albert Baylis' book *On the Way to Jesus: A Journey through the Bible* (Portland, Oreg.: Multnomah Press, 1986), Karen Lee-Thorp's work *The Story of Stories*, rev. ed. (Colorado Springs, Colo.: NavPress, 1995), and J. Sidlow Baxter's *Explore the Book* (Grand Rapids, Mich.: Zondervan Publishing House, Academie Books, 1960).

> True. . . . And on His robe and on His thigh He
> has a name written, "KING OF KINGS, AND
> LORD OF LORDS." (Rev. 19:11a, 16)

Before you see Jesus as He is, in His glory and splendor, one question begs an answer right now. Is Jesus *your* King of Kings and Lord of Lords today?

Through the many crossroads we have met in this study, it all boils down to one question. Jesus is Lord in Scripture—but is He Lord in your heart?

If He is not Lord to the degree you would like, get to know Him better. For once you know Him, you'll discover courage and confidence you never thought possible. And the best place to find Him is in the pages of His excellent Word.

———————◆———————

Heavenly Father,

   Thank You for Christ Jesus, whom You have made the author and finisher of our faith. Thank You for His finished work. Thank You that at every crossroad of our lives He is there with us and has overcome every trial we will ever encounter. Thank You that He will come some-day as King over all who would call themselves king and Lord above all who would say they are lord. Thank You for giving Him that place of preeminence and prominence.

   Father, we would ask that You would make Him as preeminent and prominent in our lives as You have made Him in all the words of Moses and the prophets and the Psalms—in all Your holy Word. We pray these things for Jesus' sake. Amen.

 Living Insights STUDY ONE

Embedded in prophecies, hidden behind analogies, and tucked into types, Christ permeates the Old Testament. Then in the Gospels He parades in full view, only to disappear into the clouds at the end. Over in Acts and the Epistles, He reaches down from heaven into the hearts of His disciples who carry His touch to the world. Finally, in Revelation, He gallops into full view again, this time as conquering King of Kings.

The Bible exudes Christ. But does He have that same prominence in your life? Do people see Him in your loving actions? Do they watch you model His values and His teaching? Do others feel His heartbeat in your words? Do they know He is Lord because He is King of your life?

If you answered no to any of these questions, then, in the space provided, confess any areas that fall short, and express your earnest desire to make Christ the Lord of every part of your life.

_____

_____

_____

_____

_____

_____

_____

_____

_____

 Living Insights STUDY TWO

Congratulations, you've made it! The last Living Insight. Getting here probably hasn't been easy for most of you. Many of the truths and questions you've encountered on these crossroads have been very, very hard, perhaps even painful to deal with. But now you're finished—almost. Before you go, would you do just one more thing?

Go treat yourself to some ice cream. Really! That's your assignment for this Living Insight. Buy yourself the chocolatiest, creamiest, biggest banana split supreme you can find—or whatever kind of wonderful dessert you enjoy. You've earned it. Will you do that?

When you do, let it be a reminder from us of how much we appreciate your effort to follow Christ at the crossroads of your life.

Bon appétit!

BOOKS FOR PROBING FURTHER

Crossroads. Challenging, risky, often painful, always shapers of character. We've walked through many of them in our study together and have found, to our relief, that Christ is there beside us in each one. We have felt Him tenderly freeing the woman caught in adulterous shame, softly smoothing the frustrated lines in Martha's anxious brow, unashamedly weeping at Lazarus' fresh grave. We've been pierced by His pain in Gethsemane and stung by His severity with the hypocrites.

But now, as we close our guide and prepare for something new, we come to yet another critical juncture—the crossroad of completion. On one path, you can choose to efficiently file away and forget the information you have gathered; on the other, you can live out what you have learned. Christ is at this crossroad too, but the choice is ultimately yours.

If you would choose the path of commitment, the following books will serve as guideposts for you. In this and in all your future crossroads, we bid you Godspeed!

> Two roads diverged in a wood, and I—
> I took the one less traveled by,
> And that has made all the difference.[1]

Ashcroft, Mary Ellen. *Temptations Women Face*. Downers Grove, Ill.: InterVarsity Press, 1991.

Augsburger, David. *Caring Enough to Confront*. Revised edition. Ventura, Calif.: GL Publications, Regal Books, 1981.

Bayly, Joseph. *The Last Thing We Talk About*. Revised edition. Elgin, Ill.: David C. Cook Publishing Co., 1973.

Campolo, Anthony, Jr. *The Success Fantasy*. Wheaton, Ill.: SP Publications, Victor Books, 1980.

---

1. Robert Frost, "The Road Not Taken," in *Poems That Live Forever*, comp. Hazel Felleman (New York, N.Y.: Doubleday, 1965), p. 317.

Conway, Jim. *Adult Children of Legal or Emotional Divorce.* Downers Grove, Ill.: InterVarsity Press, 1990.

Crabb, Larry. *Men and Women: Enjoying the Difference.* Grand Rapids, Mich.: Zondervan Publishing House, 1991.

Dobson, James C. *Love Must Be Tough.* Waco, Tex.: Word Books, 1983.

Eisenman, Tom L. *Temptations Men Face.* Downers Grove, Ill.: Inter-Varsity Press, 1990.

Friesen, Garry, with J. Robin Maxson. *Decision Making and the Will of God.* Portland, Oreg.: Multnomah Press, 1980.

Howard, J. Grant. *The Trauma of Transparency.* Portland, Oreg.: Multnomah Press, 1979.

Lucado, Max. *In the Eye of the Storm.* Dallas, Tex.: Word Publishing, 1991.

Lutzer, Erwin W. *Failure: The Back Door to Success.* Chicago, Ill.: Moody Press, 1975.

Murray, Andrew. *Christ Is All.* London, England: Collins Publishing Group, Marshall Pickering, 1990.

Rausch, David A. *A Legacy of Hatred.* Second edition. Grand Rapids, Mich.: Baker Book House, 1990.

Richmond, Gary. *The Divorce Decision.* Waco, Tex.: Word Books, 1988.

Swindoll, Charles R. *Encourage Me.* Portland, Oreg.: Multnomah Press, 1982.

———. *Simple Faith.* Dallas, Tex.: Word Publishing, 1991.

Timmer, John. *God of Weakness: How God Works through the Weak Things of the World.* Grand Rapids, Mich.: Zondervan Publishing House, 1988.

White, Jerry. *Choosing Plan A in a Plan B World.* Colorado Springs, Colo.: NavPress, 1987.

Yancey, Philip. *Disappointment with God.* Grand Rapids, Mich.: Zondervan Publishing House, 1988.

———. *Where Is God When It Hurts?* Grand Rapids, Mich.: Zondervan Publishing House, 1977.

Some of the books listed may be out of print and available only through a library. For those currently available, please contact your local Christian bookstore. Books by Charles R. Swindoll may be obtained through Insight for Living, as well as some books by other authors. Just call the IFL office that serves you

NOTES

NOTES

ORDERING INFORMATION

CHRIST AT THE CROSSROADS

If you would like to order additional study guides, purchase the cassette series that accompanies this guide, or request our product catalogs, please contact the office that serves you.

United States and International locations:
Insight for Living
Post Office Box 69000
Anaheim, CA 92817-0900

1-800-772-8888, 24 hours a day, 7 days a week
(714) 575-5000, 8:00 A.M. to 4:30 P.M., Pacific time, Monday to Friday

Canada:
Insight for Living Ministries
Post Office Box 2510
Vancouver, BC, Canada V6B 3W7

1-800-663-7639, 24 hours a day, 7 days a week

Australia:
Insight for Living, Inc.
General Post Office Box 2823 EE
Melbourne, VIC 3001, Australia

(03) 9877-4277, 8:30 A.M. to 5:00 P.M., Monday to Friday

World Wide Web:
www.insight.org

Study Guide Subscription Program
Study guide subscriptions are available. Please call or write the office nearest you to find out how you can receive our study guides on a regular basis.